AF492532

THE SOCCER PARENT HANDBOOK

Scott Martin and Chris Mumford

DEDICATION

Melissa, thank you for joining me in life and this crazy world of soccer. To my sons, Sammy and Joe, you've inspired me to look more closely at the youth soccer landscape and leave it better than I found it. And to all the players who have ever called me "Coach" and the supportive families I've encountered along the way, thank you. This one's for you.
Scott Martin

I am so grateful to my son Eli and daughter Alexi who brought me back to my childhood game which taught me so much about life. I so appreciate my wife Joelle for co-piloting in this strange and wonderful journey. Finally, I want to thank those parents who were beacons of peace amongst the chaos of the sidelines. You know who you are...
Chris Mumford

CONTENTS

Who This Book Is For

As a parent, nothing beats the unmatched joy of watching your child make a difference by scoring that amazing goal, making that perfect pass, or saving a goal to win the match. Our hearts swell and we get misty-eyed. But, navigating the soccer industrial complex is really hard...

This book is for intentional parents who want their kids to be the best versions of themselves on the soccer pitch and in life. The game can teach the mindset, process, and skills needed to be successful in life. These elements can drive your child's success in life by providing a foundation of creativity, grit, and confidence.

There is a lot of noise in youth soccer; just listen to the sidelines of a weekend game. Having never done it before, parents and kids are trying to figure it all out in real-time. The game and coaching have changed dramatically in the last 10 years. It can be confusing and frustrating.

For these reasons, parents need to know what they don't know and educate themselves. They need to be open to new, innovative ways to improve rather than settling for the ways soccer has always been done. You have to be willing to try new things to "hack the system."

This book is designed to educate you on the most you need to know in as few words as possible. The truth is that your child will need to be 10% different in order to be successful. We are going to pitch you on unique ways to help your child be different. We will make the case in short chapters, then you decide. Read these chapters again over the years as needs will change as your child matures.

Our most important credential is that we are soccer parents writing for soccer parents. Our children have played at all levels. We have coached and played at different youth levels and colleges.

Chris Mumford is a co-founder at the Accelerator School, a soccer-focused middle and high school with locations in the US and Spain. He is a professor of innovation at UNC-Chapel Hill where he teaches sports entrepreneurship. Chris is a career advisor to men's and women's professional soccer players. He is the publisher of the Premier League Guide and hosts and produces podcasts on the Premier League, La Liga, and Serie A. A former youth coach, Chris has a son and daughter in youth soccer. He played soccer at UNC-Chapel Hill.

Scott Martin is the author of Revitalizing Real Madrid: The Tactics and Stats behind Zinedine Zidane's Success and co-founder of The Football Legacy Magazine. He's also a Senior Analyst at Total Football Analysis primarily covering La Liga and Real Madrid, Match Analyst for Vélez Club de Fútbol in Spain, and a youth soccer coach for Charlotte Soccer Academy. A former collegiate assistant coach at his alma mater, Belmont Abbey College, Scott has nearly a decade of coaching experience. He currently lives in the Charlotte metroplex area with his wife and two sons.

Collaborators: We are so grateful to **Anson Dorrance** for his grand insights. **Tom Byer** crystallizes the missing pieces in early childhood soccer. **Skip Gilbert** shares his experiences as a soccer parent and administrator. **Sam Mewis** discusses personal development. **Cari Roccaro** elaborates on soccer's mental game and mental health. **Heath Pearce** shares his vision for the youth soccer landscape. **Gary Buete** talks about his experiences as a soccer parent and club CEO. Finally, friend **John Kerr** shares his views on youth development and the college pathway. **Heather Waters** is a former D1 athlete and soccer mom extraordinaire. **Jamie Brackpool's** original cover designs are much appreciated.

SECTION ONE:
Reframing the Mindset

Realistic Expectations and Goals

The truth is soccer is an unfair game…there are so few goals. The better team can lose. One mistake can lead to a win or loss. Setbacks are often and inevitable. Coaches choose players that they want.

The reality is that soccer is a great teacher because life is also unfair. It prepares your children to deal with setbacks, unfair outcomes, and subjective bosses.

There will be a beginning, middle, and end of your child's competitive soccer playing. Most players' competitive careers end earlier than they want. At all levels, I have met players who would have liked to have played longer or at a higher level. For nearly all players, competitive soccer ends before 18 or 21 years old. Ours did. Time is finite. What are you going to do to maximize the experience?

Here is our take: Focusing only on winning is bad for youth development. The parents want to win because of self-validation. The coaches want to win for better career opportunities. The clubs want to win to gain prestige or increased membership. These are all understandable. But, it's the kids who lose out. Here are the reasons.

1. The outcome of a game depends on many variables with 22 players on the pitch who average ~5 minutes of ball possession. We teach our kids to value outcomes that they cannot control.
2. When winning is paramount, youth players often play not to lose. They fear losing. Players are more conservative and less willing to try new moves to get better.
3. When winning is the only goal, losing leads to a loss of confidence which creates a vicious circle of decreased performance.
4. Parents feel compelled to coach their kids from the sideline. Players tend to seize up when they have multiple authority figures telling them what to do during a game.

We find that some parents confuse winning with their child getting better. On the sidelines, you hear parents yelling at their kids, other players, and referees. Parents see and hear what other parents are saying. This behavior can easily turn into a negative environment. Creating fear on the pitch rarely leads to a positive outcome. Postgame comments to children turn into times that the kids dread and want to avoid.

We have seen a large number of kids drop out of soccer because they experienced burnout. The truth is that they likely got tired of the win-at-all-costs atmosphere as their confidence was chipped away and, as a result, their performance did not keep up with their peers. Much of the burnout is often self-inflicted due to pressures on themselves while fanned by those around them.

As parents, we want to help our children cope with the pressures of youth soccer rather than adding to the tension and anxiety. For that to happen, we must first acknowledge our own anxieties. Gary Buete, the CEO of North Carolina FC Youth, recommends starting with the way we view the game: "A lot of parents watch the game with the hope their son or daughter doesn't mess up…Know they're going to have days where they're great, they're going to have days where they mess up. Understand that process, that it's a long journey. There's a lot of time to do the right thing and get better."

Winning isn't a given and performances waver. With that in mind, we can approach the game from a more informed position and help our kids see the game from an alternative mindset.

So what is the alternative? Let's examine the building blocks to success in soccer. Some of these are controllable while others are not.

Little control
Athleticism
This quality is largely genetic though speed and agility training can alter by up to 20% in our estimation. Size matters some but speed and agility matter much more over time.

Desire to Win
The best players do have a desire to win in spades. They don't need

any external motivation to win.

Work Rate Successful players just want to train more. They go to the fields early or stay late.

More control
Process Mindset

Successful players buy into the notion that success is a process, not an outcome. Training is the journey to be appreciated.

Technical Skills

These learned attributes include first touches, ball striking, and dribbling moves. The skills have to be practiced daily at home or outside of regular soccer training.

Anticipation

The better players can see plays developing 0.1 seconds faster than others. This comes from watching lots of games and regularly playing, especially pickup.

Adaptation

Players learn how to evolve their game based on real-time information and training. They quickly change to current conditions.

Joy

The most successful players just love being out on the pitch. They want to try new things and want more challenges.

Flow

The great players can regularly reach that state of mind where everything feels natural. They see the play and know what to do easily. Michael Jordan spoke about feeling tension but not undue pressure.

Grit

Kids who can actively learn from a setback and bounce back quickly are at a huge advantage. In addition, they know how to grind out a solid performance when they don't have the flow.

Confidence Management

The most successful players make mistakes, learn from them, and then forget about the mistakes.

"Selective forgetfulness" is helpful in creating a virtuous circle of confidence. The lack of confidence is the greatest enemy of the player.

In short, encourage your player to be aware of the factors that they have little control over while being intentional about the aspects they can control. In the next chapter, we do a deeper dive into these areas.

I think when we start to use words like "expectations", we've already crossed a line. I think if all of a sudden you're imposing that on your kid, you've really crossed the line.

I think what we should do is we should wrap our arms around our kids because, as you will discover, as Melissa and I have already learned, they're going to be in and out of your home in a flash and you're going to really regret every minute you didn't spend with them. Rather than live with that regret, you should make sure every aspect of their lives is overwhelmingly positive, at least from your perspective.

Now does that mean you coddle them and protect them from pain and failure? No. But when they do experience pain and failure, you let them know, "Hey, guess what? You're gonna be okay." And if they're experiencing pain and failure in sport, what an incredible environment for them to fail in.

Because you know what? It doesn't matter. It doesn't matter if you suck at soccer. "You want to be any good? All right. Was it painful to get hammered 9-0 in that game and you want to be better? Well, then, hey, it's up to you. Then you get to make decisions on who you are and where you want to go." But if all of a sudden, we as parents are starting to have these expectations, now we're going in the wrong direction.

Let's make sure our kids are educated. For me, that's one of the primary missions that we have, to educate our kids when they're in our homes, teach them core values, how you treat people, how you behave, what's your character's like. Those are our missions, if you're spiritual, making sure they have a good spiritual education as well, I think those are our priorities.

And yeah, sports are so much fun and as long as that's the ambition for every parent with their kids, then I think they're going in the right direction. I think if we do start to use words like expectation, it's like we've hired a consulting firm, to raise our children.

No, no, no, no, no. We can get a lot simpler than that. Love your kid. Take care of them. Protect them from the chaos of the universe.

But protect them from failure? No. Protect them from failure or pain in sports, no. What a great environment to experience failure and then decide who you are. You didn't like that [failure]? Well, do you want to do something about it? Yeah, spend some time [training]. So for me, it's not that complex?

- Anson Dorrance

UNC Women's Soccer Coach and World Cup Champion Coach with the US Women's National Team (1991)

Summary
1. Soccer is unfair…and so is life, which makes the soccer field a perfect environment for experiencing setbacks.
2. Players have little control in some areas of the sport, especially athleticism.
3. Other areas offer far more control, such as a process mindset, technical skill, confidence management, and "selective forgetfulness.

What It Takes

In this chapter, we explore what it takes to help your player be the best version of themselves and how you can keep sane. Soccer success relies on so many variables outside the control of your player and you. As a parent, the best thing you can do is to create the best environment for your player to be successful.

~~Winning is Everything~~

Over the last 30 years, I have learned to detest the cliche "Winners never quit. Quitters never win."

The truth is that Winners always adapt. If something isn't working, they try something else. The faster your player learns how to adapt, the better they will perform. If that adaptation is for your player to quit soccer and try another sport, then let them try.

In youth development soccer, winning is overrated. No one will remember whether a game was won or lost a year ago. Sure, it's nice if it happens. As parents, we care if our player is better this month versus last month, not if she won the game. Parents should stay focused on long-term development rather than a short-term win. Focusing on winning games encourages players to do only what they have done before without trying new things. They play conservatively. It teaches a mindset of playing not to lose rather than win.

An unfortunate consequence is that many youth games become this frenzied screaming match between the parents of opposing teams. The players are already stressed and complaining that parents don't help the environment. As a parent, it's hard not to get sucked up into the negative energy. The player is there to get better, not necessarily to win every game. Wait until she/he is in college or the pros for that to happen.

"My daughter wasn't doing well in soccer and quit competitive soccer for a while to try other sports. I wanted her to find something where she would give a 100% effort. In time, she came back to soccer. She is all in. I want her to live her dream, not mine. I've had plenty of chances in the past. What is done is done. It's too much of a burden on them to live my dream and their dream.

In fact, I ask my kids every month if they want to quit soccer. I say that it costs a lot of money and time. They can do whatever else they want if they fully commit. For now, they tell me no every month. With this question, I'm confident that the kids are living their dream, not mine." Chris Mumford

To increase their chance of success, the player and family should set achievable goals with a plan and specific tasks to do.

Perfection is Overrated

In soccer, the objective of never making a mistake is short-sighted. Players should be encouraged to try new things and make mistakes in an effort to improve. Players who try to be perfect will tend to only do things that have worked before in previous conditions. There is an unwillingness to try to do something differently even though it may lead to a better outcome. Encourage your player to try new things, make mistakes, and learn. Of course, they want to avoid making the same mistake over and over again. The faster they learn, then the faster they will improve.

The other negative consequence of trying to be perfect is that the mindset slowly destroys confidence. Sometimes, you can do something perfectly and things still don't work out. The player is disappointed because the outcome didn't match the expectation. These situations lead to self-doubt and ultimately declining confidence and bitterness.

Accept Reality

The first step is to accept reality for what it is and be able to understand how it is different from what you want reality to be. This is an idea that is easy to understand but really hard to do. Are you and your player able to step back and look at things as objectively as possible? It takes practice.

For the player, we often ask them to imagine themselves as two separate versions: player and coach. The player version just plays and finds a flow. In their self-coaching mode, how do they imagine that they are pulling back and coaching themselves without all the emotion? Imagine what advice they would give to a younger player. Parents can introduce their kids to the idea and discuss how the player can give positive feedback to themselves.

Adaptability

There is a reason why humans are the most successful species on earth. It is not because we are faster, stronger, or tougher. We have adapted to the ever-changing reality better than other species. Introduce your player to the idea of observing what is happening around them and changing their actions quickly. They may have to take a step back if they are playing against a much faster player. Or they may have to adjust to what a new coach wants and play a different position. How can you cultivate a culture of your player embracing change when it is needed?

Successful players adjust to changed field conditions or the opposing player's movements. Coaches modify tactics at halftime based on the opposing team's play. Insanity is defined as expecting a different outcome while always doing the same thing, sticking to the same old method when it doesn't work in the current conditions. Adapted effort is what is needed.

Probabilistic Mindset

Actions do not guarantee success. Actions can increase the likelihood of success. This view is called the probabilistic mindset. For example, a better team will beat another lesser team 7 out of 10 times. On any given Sunday match, a lesser team can still win. A ball can bounce a funny way or an accidental handball in the box may happen. That's why we still play the game.

The better team's coaches and players can prepare and work more intelligently to increase those chances to 8 out of 10. The truth is that your player has a low probability of playing college ball at age 10. There are many actions, such as more technical and speed/agility training, that can improve those chances, but not guarantee them. The college coach may not have a need for a player in your child's position the year your child applies.

It's important for your player to understand that there are no guarantees in soccer, or life, but you can work hard to improve the chances. Persistence over long periods will enable success.

Growth Mindset

Traditionally, a child will say that "I am not good at _____." For example, I'm not good at math. I'm not good with my non-dominant foot. Or I can't play this position. The truth is that there are players that are more naturally talented. However, intentional practice over sustained periods can help players overcome most shortcomings. In the world of education, this is called the Growth Mindset. Focused hard work is the basic building block of all successful players. Players don't need to self-limit what they can and cannot do. High work rates fueled by passion and a reflective mind should not be underestimated.

> **Most successful athletes failed, missed cuts, or lost a spot on a team. Athletes don't want their 11/12/13/14 to be the most successful time of their careers.**
>
> **-Heather Waters**
> **Former D1 Athlete and Soccer Mom Extraordinaire**

Managing Expectations

Help your player establish realistic expectations. Create intermediate goals that they can act on instead of outcomes. For example, instead of scoring one goal a game, make five sensible runs into the box to create scoring opportunities. Invest the time in understanding the game and what each position does so you can understand how to establish realizable, intermediate goals. This book is a step in the right direction. Make no more than one or two goals a game, three goals weekly and monthly. Change goals once they are consistently achieved.

> **You have to be patient. I don't think that there's a magic button. Development is a marathon, not a sprint. It's not like you figure things out and it just moves so quickly. So parents need to know there's a certain degree of patience that needs to take place as well. That's why I like that analogy of the marathon versus the sprint. They have to understand what development looks like and why some players develop quicker than other players and focus on that. But for me, it comes down to expectations, always.**
>
> **-Tom Byer**
> **Founder of Soccer Starts at Home and Internationally Acclaimed Youth Development Guru**

Goal Setting and Planning

Setting clear, achievable goals is a key to success. Let's examine how to frame the goals. In youth soccer, most players set overarching goals like be a consistent starter, move up to the next level team, play college ball, or win the cup. It's good to have a simple goal or outcome.

It is equally important to have process goals to support the overarching goals. These are action-oriented goals. For example, for the player that wants to become a consistent starter, complete one additional weekly training and 20 minutes of self-training daily. Translate the big goal into weekly or daily goals that can be checked once completed.

Parents should help players develop a season plan of the overarching goals, then break it into weekly and daily goals. The plan doesn't have to be longer than one page. The parent and player should review the plan monthly to see how the outcome compares to the plan. Change the plan when needed. Plan the work. Work the plan. Pivot when needed.

It's a Process

The process is executing the plan and adjusting. Encourage the player to enjoy the process: the training, spending time with teammates, and just being on the ball. Remind the player that there is a beginning, middle, and end to everything. Most likely, the soccer experience is as good as it's going to get. There will be peaks and valleys in terms of interest, injuries, and improvement. The hard part is to moderate the high and low points as a player's identity is so tied up in soccer performance. Keep in mind the top priority is to help keep the joy in the game.

> **We find that the more active that the parent is in the early stages of development, the better appreciation and understanding they have. They're more likely to not be that stereotypical kind of soccer moms, soccer dads screaming at the kid from the sidelines because they have a better appreciation. They understand the game better and that's why it's very important.**
>
> **-Tom Byer**

Repetition

Multiple repetitions are the absolutely necessary elements for success. Your player has to get in more reps than their peers to get better. There is simply no substitute. These reps include club soccer practice, self-training, private training, pick-up, and offseason training. How can your player enjoy getting more reps than their peers? John Kerr, the Duke University Men's Soccer Coach, finds intentional training a necessity for success, noting, "just like the 10,000-hour rule, technical development is not an accident. It doesn't happen just because you hope it to happen. You've got to get out there and work on your game." Club soccer training alone will not be sufficient.

Here is the trick: does your player have the motivation over many years to be intentionally training, assuming some breaks?

You will have to read the room to see if the desire is there. Most likely, your desire and pushing them will not work over the long term. Their desire will not be successful enough if you don't support them enough. The goal is to support their desire and keep it joyful. There is a beginning, middle, and end to everything, especially soccer. Support your player at the level that they want to be successful and joyful. Instead of over-scheduling, let their self-motivation dictate the pace.

Each player is different. Chris's son was always self-motivated and could never get enough training. His daughter's interest ebbed and flowed. He and his wife supported their son's obsession while encouraging their daughter to take a break from competitive soccer and pursue other sports with a passion. In the end, she came back to the game of competitive soccer though they encouraged her to do other things.

> **Danielle Egan Reyna and Claudio Reyna's son, Gio, who's now playing in the Champions League and is one of the best American players in his age group of all-time, was allowed to play AAU basketball right up through U14.**
>
> **Why? Because the parents wanted him to enjoy his life.**
>
> **So they don't have to specialize young. They just have to love what they're doing, and then that's going to be the catalyst for them to get to their potential in some sport.**
>
> **-Anson Dorrance**

One note: it is hard to be an objective parent. Objective defined as understanding how your player is relative to others. Or objective defined as being able to step back and not say anything when it is clear that your player doesn't want any advice. Be prepared to make mistakes and learn from them.

Keep in mind your child is playing a game where 22 players are trying to kick the ball into a net. There are some valuable life lessons that can be learned, as well as a lifelong passion gained.

Confidence Management

The best players are described as having grit or being resilient. They have setbacks and learn from them. Confidence management is the habit that is usually the final piece in becoming a great player from a good player. Like everything, confidence has its ebbs and flows. A good performance in one match can turn around a whole season. However, this is the least coached area in soccer and, likely, all sports. While some players may have more natural confidence than others, confidence management is a skill that can be learned in the right environment. As a parent, you can develop an environment to facilitate confidence acquisition. Have honest conversations about what happens in training and matches. Support them when they talk about what worked and what did not work.

The fastest way to create a vicious circle of downward spiraling confidence is by having fear on the field, afraid to make mistakes and hearing angry parents or the coach.

> **I think confidence is one of the hardest things to talk about because it's so individual. Having been a teenage girl, I would be hard-pressed to meet a teenage girl who doesn't have insecurities.**
> **But I think something that has resonated with me over the years is that my confidence is mine. No matter what a coach or the media says about me, nobody should be able to take or give that to me. It's something that I need to nourish and hold onto myself.**
>
> **Confidence comes from being prepared, it comes from doing extra, it comes from this kind of inner voice that reinforces when you do something good, and it's definitely tricky. And I'm not confident all the time, but I like to think that I'm in control of that and that somebody on the outside can't take it away or can't give it back. It has to come from someplace inside.**
>
> **It's tough because I realize I just said that nobody should be able to give or take it, but you have to kind of teach that positive reinforcement. When I think about my parents, like my mom is so...she thinks I did well,**

no matter what I did, like I could have scored an own goal and she would blame somebody else. I think that kind of blind faith in me helps when I'm down, for sure, like knowing that I have that support no matter what, it helps.

I think my dad is much more willing to point out critiques that he has and that balance of my parents is kind of this perfect storm that I know not everybody has. So it's kind of unfair to say you and your partner should make this perfect storm of confidence for your kids, but I do think that providing positive reinforcement with a balance of criticism when it's necessary, or when you think that they can give more, is important. I guess I don't have the secret ingredient of how to make a kid who's self-sufficient and confident. I think that kids just have to learn it and grow into it.

-Sam Mewis

US Women's National Team and Manchester City Midfielder, World Cup Champion (2019) and 2020 U.S. Soccer Female Player of the Year

Anticipation

"Skate to where the puck is going, not where it has been." Wayne Gretzy

This habit can be a superpower and great equalizer, especially if you are not a super athlete. Anticipation is seeing an action unfolding and correctly guessing what will happen next. Help your player be aware of their surroundings by looking around them and forecast the play that is going to happen. As with everything, there is only one way to get better: practice. Watch games together and ask your player what is going to happen next. Encourage your player to constantly look around them or shoulder check so they are situationally aware.

Most likely, your player will compete against others who are bigger or faster. However, if your player is able to process what will happen faster than others, then they will get to where the ball will be before others. Soccer is a game of being in the right place at the right time.

Giving Advice

Generally, it's best to avoid talking immediately after a game when emotions (including yours) are high. Give time for your player and you to process what happened. Focus on listening. Let the car ride home be quiet. The player will open up if they want.

Determine if they only want to be heard. Evaluate if they want your advice. As an analogy, sometimes partners want to be heard about a problem versus you helping them solve a problem. In the best of all possibilities, your player asks you your opinion. As a parent, controlling the urge to volunteer advice is the hardest thing to do. But, you will have more credibility if you hold back sometimes.

After ample time, ask the following:

1. What positive things occurred during the match?
2. Where there are opportunities for improvement? Let them talk about their mistakes without judgment. Acknowledge their feelings as legitimate.
3. What can they learn from those mistakes?

After you hear their thoughts, you can share what you think if it is appropriate. If you're not sure, ask follow-up questions. The role is more of one as a facilitator to help them process the event rather than an expert coach. If you have opinions, express them positively in how you phrase them. Be candid. Don't offer false compliments as your player will pick up on this tendency and discount your positive feedback. Make them earn the positive feedback. Rephrase "You should do this _____" to "I see an opportunity in you doing this _____. What do you think?" I often use the qualifier, "My take is _____" or "I don't know" to indicate that other possibilities exist or I don't know the answer to everything.

Try not to repeat yourself once you have made your points. Encourage your player to talk about mistakes, learn from them and then forget about the mistakes. A recipe for success is to learn from the mistakes rather than let them haunt your player. Remind them that it is good to try new things and make mistakes. Learn from them and move on. This method is the best teacher.

Some players are better than others in hearing advice from their parents. Your job is to read the room. Work on when is the right time to share your comments or not. Your player's interest may ebb and flow as they get older. Remember the goal is to help them get better. If you need to vent, talk to your spouse or a friend about it.

This overall approach will help your player deal with setbacks and manage their confidence. Many great players are described as resilient or having grit. Somewhere down the line, they learned from their mistakes without wrecking their confidence.

Summary

1. Have a positive realist mindset that adapts to the ever-changing scenarios of the game.
2. Growth mindsets help players see mistakes as opportunities for development and correction through intentional practice. Failure's not an enemy, but an ally. A growth mindset is essential in confidence management.
3. Have a plan. Start with the end in mind, then build backward to create a development plan. Tailor expectations to understand development is a process that requires reps, both technically and tactically.

Physical Growth

In the US, the system favors the bigger, athletic players. The US college system is a perfect example, though that is changing. If you visit other countries, the players are smaller, blazing-fast, and highly technically skilled. Changes in size will likely have the most impact on your player from age 13-17 depending on the gender. Some are bigger as prepubescent players while others hit puberty earlier. All other things equal, the bigger and faster prepubescent player will do better and make team rosters easier, especially in the early club years.

The reality is that you cannot change this much. There is an old Chinese saying: you can't make a rice plant grow faster by trying to pull it toward the sky. However, you can manage the process.

First, let's discuss the baseline. Evaluate the size and how athletic your spouse and you are. Consider those attributes with your parents and uncles/aunts. According to the Mayo Clinic, there is no proven way to forecast a child's height. There are several options for providing a reasonable guess which is generally +/- 2 inches:

1. Boys: Add father's height + mother's height + 5 inches. Then, divide by 2.

2. Girls: Add father's height + mother's height - 5 inches. Then, divide by 2.

3. Double a girl's height at 18 months age and a boy's height at 24 months age.

4. Some clubs and pediatricians can also provide an estimate by measuring the child's age, height, sitting height, and femur length.

If your spouse and you have different ethnicities and gene pools, then your children will possibly be bigger and faster. Compare the diet your spouse and you had when you were children against the diet your players are having. Recall when your spouse and you reached puberty. Evaluating these factors will provide a potential development timeline for your player.

Let's get back to the fact that you can't influence growth significantly with the exceptions of diet, stress management, and sleep. Chris's son tried everything including hanging upside down for extended periods. He has since settled on sleeping as much as he can and eating a healthy diet. His daughter settled on a healthy diet.

A player's reaction to their growth profile can significantly impact their playing career.

Smaller players

These players will need to double down on their technical and mental training. They will need as many touches on the ball as they will enjoy. Moreover, they can watch games (ideally with their parents) to learn how their position is played by the best.

In the prepubescent stage, speed and agility training will help modestly as there are some improvements in running form. In practice, the training will help develop good habits when they have muscular development.

Encouraging a strong work ethic is important as the journey is long and should be enjoyable. In the early years, their efforts will be rewarded more quickly. Teaching good habits in being "coachable," responsive, and appreciative of a coach's input is also very helpful.

The goal is for your smaller player to exhibit a very strong work ethic, a good foundation in technical training, and be coachable. Though Sam Mewis was always one of the tallest players on her team, her message to smaller players was overwhelmingly positive: "There are lots of players who are late bloomers, so patience is really important and so is not giving up on the sport. If you feel like you're lagging behind or too small, know that some of the best players I know are really small, and having patience and believing that your hard work will pay off is really important." This profile is important in long-term success.

Some clubs, and sport science in general, are embracing the idea of grouping players by physiological age rather than chronological age. Sometimes, it does not match up. In 2018, US Soccer introduced the concept of bio-banding which allows an older player to train and play with a younger team, generally a year younger. In the beginning, some families balked as players only wanted to play with kids their chronological age, in part due to pride and staying with kids they knew.

Chris's local club suggested that his son bio-band as he was undersized at the time but had the right profile. Other families rejected the notion. They signed up based on the recommendations of experienced coaches who looked out for his development. Two years later, he rejoined his age group once his late-onset of puberty happened. In retrospect, his lack of size became a significant advantage as he knew he had to train more and work on other qualities to compete.

If your player matches the profile above, you may want to chat with the coach or director about whether bio-banding is a good fit.

Larger players

These players and families are generally relieved that they have the starting spots. However, the growth spurt will stop at some point and other players will likely physically catch up. In our experiences, we have seen larger players at 12 or 13 years old become undersized players when they reached 17 or 18 years old.

They didn't match the ideal profile because they did not work on speed and agility training, technical, or mental skills. It was easy to get complacent when they started on the team with less effort. Most high-level teams have a large number of athletic, bigger players who lack the technical skills and work ethic to play at the next level.

> **One of the things I say all the time is the best players at 11 are hardly ever the best players at 18. The big, strong, fast girls when they're 10 or 11, it's easy for them not to work on some of the basics of the game and technique...you've seen where the greatest player in the**

> **world at 11, because of size and speed and strength, ends up not being able to go on and play at another level while those who have been the smallest players come out being the best players in the end.**
>
> **-Gary Buete**
> **CEO of North Carolina FC Youth**

The best practice is to educate your player that their size will likely only be a temporary advantage and that agility, technical, and mental skills training will be the long-term difference makers. As John Kerr says, "you can't cheat the system by not working on your skills, whatever category you're in."

In short, both smaller and larger players should work on the same things given that the destination is the same but the path is different.

Sleep

Everyone knows that sleep is really important but most folks tend to let bad habits happen. The American Academy of Sleep Medicine has recommended that children aged 6–12 years should regularly sleep 9–12 hours per 24 hours and teenagers aged 13–18 years should sleep 8–10 hours per 24 hours. Clearly, every child is different but don't assume that your child will get sufficient recovery with the minimum recommended hours. Let's do an example if your child needs to be up by 7am.

Kids aged 6-12: bedtime - 7pm-10pm

Teenagers 13-18 years: bedtime - 9pm-11pm

As you know, this is hard in the era of screens and smartphones which are designed to be addictive. Let's get into sleep science.

The truth is that training alone does not make a player better. Training + Sleep makes a player better according to sleep scientist, Matthew Walker, Professor of Neurology and Psychology at UC Berkeley and Founder of the Center for Sleep Science.

Walker explains that fine motor skills (like soccer training) are learned while awake and then replayed or rehearsed at 20 times the original speed in the brain when sleeping. This action leads to the sculpting of neural pathways so the brain and body are able to normalize those movements. In an interview with Joe Rogan, he elaborates that - with practice and sleep - fine motor skill performance is 20-30% better in skill performance compared to the end of the practice session the previous day.

Sleep is the greatest legal performance-enhancing drug in sport.

With good sleep habits, skill learning is maximized, but also muscles can fully recover. If your sleep time drops to six hours, then the time to physical exhaustion drops by 30%. For example, if your child trains for a 90 minute game, she/he could be physically exhausted after 63 minutes. With insufficient sleep, muscles are not able to fully recover from the micro-tears associated with training.

As parents, we have to be crafty to create an environment for good sleep habits. In the best of all worlds, kids turn off screens an hour before bedtime. If that is not possible, have kids wear blue-blocking glasses to allow for proper melatonin release. Greatly reducing blue light alerts the brain that it is time to go to sleep.

It may be the case that the entire household - including parents - develop a regular sleep schedule. These sacrifices for your children may end up helping your sleep, performance, and ultimate well-being.

Nutrition

We have found this to be a contentious issue amongst parents. The science is pretty clear but it runs against maximum convenience and taste. You likely know the reasoning - bad fuel generally leads to bad outcomes. But, we still give unhealthy snacks to our kids because it is easy while sugar, fat, and salt all taste good, especially together. Big food companies have spent years developing the most habit-forming foods for children and ourselves.

The general rule is to not eat foods that come in a plastic bag (except salad) or a box. If possible, avoid foods that are in the inside aisles of a grocery store, according to Michal Pollan the Professor at the UC Berkeley Graduate School of Journalism. He provides details in a short book called Food Rules: An Eater's Guide.

When speaking with professional athletes, each seemed to have a discovery moment when they realized that their food choices were undermining their desire to improve performance, Cari Roccaro among them, noting, "I would adjust my diet earlier. As a pro, you figure out what you can eat, what fuels you the best to be able to sustain running for 90 minutes at a fast pace and be super fit." Over time, they revamped their diet to align with their goals. They still splurge occasionally for salty, carb snacks or candy.

Each family has to decide what is realistic. Like sleep, parents can be crafty in subtly shifting meals to create enhanced fuel for their children. Start with swapping out one unhealthy snack/meal weekly. Good eating habits are easiest to adopt at a younger age. These changes can likely lead to a healthier outcome for our children given the current situation where ⅔ of Americans are either obese or overweight.

Summary

1. Patience is a virtue. Remember that physical growth happens on its own time. Keep in mind that sleep and nutrition will be a huge factor in growth.
2. Smaller players should take advantage of a physical disadvantage, outperforming their peers in the technical and soccer IQ sections of the game.
3. Larger players have a temporary advantage, but many rely too heavily on physical dominance at a young age. When growth spurts kick in, these players tend to fall way behind. Avoid this fall from grace by working just as hard on the technical and soccer IQ sides of the game as your smaller peers. Don't just rely on a temporary athletic advantage.

Boys vs Girls

In the younger age groups, there's not much of a difference between coaching boys vs girls. However, as the kids age, especially once they hit the teenage years, those differences are more prominent.

With that in mind, let's touch on some of the most common differences between the two and how coaches commonly differentiate their approaches.

Culture vs Social dynamics

On a collective level, the biggest difference between boys' and girls' teams comes down to how they interact with each other.

For the boys, team culture is the most important element. Guys can easily play in the same team as someone that can't stand on a social level. The guys might not talk to each other much when the ball is out of play, but, when the ball is in play, all that matters is that each player meets performance and competitiveness standards. The thing that's most damaging to a boys' team is when one or some of the players refuse to meet those standards. That's when all hell breaks loose. Acceptance within the boys' teams is very much predicated on your ability to meet a certain level of play and your willingness to compete.

It's a little bit different on the girls' side. Again, this is just our direct experience, but ask your daughter how many teammates she knocked to the ground at practice. Ask her how many times she engaged in a hard challenge against a teammate. In all likelihood, it didn't happen.

Now, don't take this to be a hard and fast rule. We've both had some ultra-competitive girls teams, as well as some boys teams that were more socially inclined and less comfortable with contact. The collective character of the team comes before any hard and fast gender distinctions, but that's where the coach must investigate what the team's expectations are and help them get to the desired endpoint.

> **Playing on a boys team in high school was the best experience I could have ever had. It took some time to understand that what happened on the court wasn't personal. When we had tryouts for the team, everyone would go get lunch afterwards. I was confused, but quickly learned that what happens in the court stays there and there are no friends during competition, but once that's over the friendship continues.**

- Heather Waters

Coachability vs Improvisation

"Coach, just tell us what to do."

That's a common thing you'll hear during a girl's practice. The downside is that frustration levels build a little bit quicker, especially when there isn't immediate success, but the upside is that girls typically understand the concepts and apply them much quicker than boys. They tend to be very coachable, to the point where some of our teams have taken one or two practices to learn fairly difficult concepts and applied them during their next game. The turnaround time is staggering, especially if the technical basics are already in place.

Boys teams tend to need a little more time in that regard. There will be more trial and error with the soccer IQ and tactical concepts. One of the reasons for this is that boys tend to rely on improvisation when their backs are up against the wall. Rather than sticking to the system and the ideas at play in the session, you will generally see boys try unnecessarily complex techniques to get out of trouble. But that's also their strength too. Once the bigger idea is finally drilled into their minds and they start to see their freedoms within the system, they will tend to use those freedoms in more intelligent ways.

The same amount of coaching, the same exercises, and the same tactical endpoint will often look very clean and structured on the girls' side and more chaotic on the boys'. In that sense, coachability and improvisation are both strengths and weaknesses for the two genders. Girls who have the confidence and talent to make greater use of improvisation can really stand out, while boys who maintain their improvisational ability while also showing greater coachability and focus on the plan will at least make a quicker start than their peers.

Collective vs Individual

Following from the coachability vs improvisation conversation, you've probably guessed that girls tend to be more collective in their approach while the boys are more individualistic. On a general level, that is a fair assessment.

Again, this goes to reinforce the point that a female player who maintains a collective approach while showing confidence and ability in her individual contributions can really shine. Fear of failure is one of the biggest hurdles for female players. The girls who can overcome that fear of individual mistakes can bring another element to her team. That aggressive mentality that drives a love of 1v1 matchups needs to be fostered by her coaches, teammates, and the parent group. Don't shame or reproach the girl for this important quality.

Since guys are more naturally individualistic, they need to train their 1v1 ability to ensure that when it's used it works more often than not. But, that said, the biggest hurdle on the guys' side of the game is showing them how the individual element fits into the collective. That's where the big picture is really important. We have to show them how they are part of this system and how the whole group functions. Then we have to bring it back to the micro-level, showing them the individual freedoms they have within the bigger picture. In that way, we're both ensuring that we protect their love of individual contribution and place them in situations where we can maximize their odds of success.

Aggression and confidence

Parents and coaches can really have a big influence here. Some of the least aggressive and confident players we've coached are the ones who are constantly berated. When they make a mistake on the field, either the coach or parents yell at the kid or make some kind of dramatic gesture to show their displeasure.

Scott once had a player who, every time she made a mistake, immediately looked to the sideline to watch her dad's reaction. The hands would fly up in the air, then he'd turn around because he couldn't look at the field. That was the image his daughter saw every time she made a mistake.

Do you know what she did? She only engaged in the simplest of actions. If there was even the slightest chance of failure, she refused to try it, which is a shame because she was a talented player.

Girls tend to show less aggression and more severe dips in confidence than boys, but it's certainly not gender exclusive.

One of Scott's former players, we'll call him Justin, spent two great years on his team. Justin was voted captain by his peers in both seasons. He was a staple in our midfield and a top player on the team.

Getting to know Justin over those two years, Scott learned about his previous experiences in the game. He had coaches who gave him very little playing time and, if he made even the slightest mistake, subbed him off immediately. There were some games where he'd go in for one or two minutes at a time and then come right back off the field and sit on the bench.

That sort of environment will damage the freedom, aggression, and confidence of any player, boy or girl. In the end, club culture and the leadership of the coach are incredibly important, as is the sense of community fostered on the parents' sideline. Yes, there can be differences between the genders, but know that all kids are going to struggle in these areas, even if there is a tough exterior.

Ultimately, they're no different than us. We all go through periods where we feel like we can conquer the world, but also times when we feel like we just can't catch a break. As parents, we want to help our kids stay focused on the task, present in the moment, and learn to navigate those tough psychological situations. Each of us plays a major role in developing our kid's mental skills. We want to teach them to assess their problems, ask the right questions, and work towards answers that get them back on track. Returning the kids to a focused and deliberate mental state is our priority, we just have to remember that it's also a skill we have to help them develop.

> **What I would love for parents to do is to raise them [their daughters] to some extent like boys in this respect...if your girl is incredibly competitive, don't make her some Caspar milk toast.**
>
> **What's really interesting about the culture is the way we raise our boys and young men. If they're extraordinarily competitive, they are lauded. They're put on a pedestal. If our girls are extraordinarily competitive within their own cultures, and I guess their homes because that's a part of their initial cultures, they're excoriated for being competitive. I think that is a huge mistake. If you have an incredibly competitive daughter, keep cheering her on...Somewhere in her environment, she has to have someone throwing their arms around her for being this competitive warrior.**
>
> **There's nothing wrong if you're a young girl, just like if you're a young boy, who wants to win everything. There's nothing wrong with that, so let's embrace our girls that are competitive. Let's give them a safe haven somewhere.**
>
> **What I would advise all parents to do is to protect their competitive girls just like they protect and laud and put on a pedestal their competitive boys.**
>
> **-Anson Dorrance**

Summary

1. The on-field culture is the primary concern for boys, whereas girls thrive when the social dynamics around the team are excellent.

2. Girls tend to view the game more collectively and are generally quicker to absorb and apply information. Boys have a tendency to show more individualistic qualities, which requires more time to train ideas but gives them an edge in improvisational ability.

3. There's very little difference between boys and girls in aggression and confidence management. They might have different triggers, such as hurtful words or the actions of a coach or teammate, but this is where we, as parents, help our kids improve their confidence management to aggressively engage the game.

Letters to Parents

This chapter's special. Rather than reading about our thoughts, we've recruited the experts to relate their experience of youth soccer. Ranging from Joelle, a soccer mom, all the way down to Sammy at the entry-level, our interviewees offer a complete timeline of the youth soccer experience.
Let's jump right into them.

Letter from Soccer Mom to Soccer Mom

Soccer for a five-year-old is obviously very different from soccer for an older kid. When my son was five, we needed something to do during a cold Chicago winter and the parks and rec soccer class at a small nearby community center seemed perfect. Flash forward to today, my son is seventeen and wants to be a professional soccer player. I never would have imagined him saying that when he was five. The discipline and dedication required to get him to even be remotely able to do this job is excessive.

My advice to parents who are considering getting their kids into soccer is to follow your child's interests. All along the way, my son was committed and devoted, despite not being the most talented on the field. We matched his energy and enthusiasm along the way.

My daughter is a different story. She showed an interest in soccer, so we followed it, signed her up for soccer teams. But she complained when it was time to go to practice, saying she felt tired or just did not want to go. She got injured often, sometimes twice during a season or a big injury that would take her out for an entire season. We would say, 'Let's find another sport! Doesn't seem like you're really into soccer." But she kept wanting to sign up for the next season.

One season she took a step back and went to a team that practiced twice a week instead of three times a week and she tried jump rope. At the beginning of jump rope season, she had an injury that prevented her from jumping for 3 months! The next season she decided to recommit to soccer.

Flash forward to today, she loves soccer and we are still following her lead. We take her to practice because she wants to go. I did push a little at times when she was younger because she seemed happy after training and games. Knowing when to push her to get to a practice was confusing and hard at times, but we did it sometimes. At thirteen, she now says she's grateful that we pushed a little. She says she loves soccer, loves the team aspect and the game.

The main advice I'd give for parents with kids showing an interest in soccer is to follow your child's lead. And if you've spent a lot of time and money on soccer for years and they suddenly want to quit, calmly say okay and think about all the emotional growth and personal development that was gained during the time spent at practice and at games.

Joelle P.
Soccer Mom and Soccer Uber Driver

Letter from a USA International to Soccer Parents

A common question [I receive] is, "did your parents put pressure on you to become really good [at soccer]and succeed?"

They really didn't.

When Kristie and I started getting called into youth national team camps, which meant that we would miss weeks of school to go and travel, sometimes to California for a week-long camp with a U15 or U17 national team, my parents would always ask, "do you want to go?" I think that for a lot of parents, that wouldn't even cross their minds. "Of course, they want to go. This is such a great opportunity. We want them to go."

My parents' perspective was, "let's make sure that this is what they want, that they're okay missing school." Every time, Kristie and I were like, "of course we want to go." There was never a doubt from us, but I just think that for my parents to be able to see the big picture and make sure that it was something we really wanted, and not just something they thought we wanted, was really important. It let Kristie and I know that we weren't being forced into anything, that if we ever chose not to pursue soccer at that level, we had that option and our parents would love us anyway.

There are so many important life lessons to be taken from soccer. If I ever have kids, my hope for my kids would be that they learn all the life lessons that I've learned. It wouldn't necessarily be that they go on to become professionals. I think that by just exposing your kids to the sport, you're doing a good thing as a parent. As long as they are learning these positive life lessons from it and not expecting that every kid is going to want to become a pro or is going to be good enough to become a pro, I think soccer is so wonderful, even if you're just playing for fun.

Most of the really, really successful players that I know are internally motivated. No matter how much your parents want you to become a professional soccer player or get a full ride to college, if that's not what the player wants or is motivated to do, maybe their motivation is elsewhere. It's really hard to make that happen for somebody else, even if it's your kid. So I would just say to trust that your kid is going to find their passion. If it's soccer, then you're going to know that and you're going to see that in them because they're going to push themselves. But if it's somewhere else, there's still a lot to get from the sport, but don't force it onto your kids.

Sam Mewis

Letter from Older Youth Player to Soccer Parents

Dear Parent,

For the past 10 years of my life, I have lived in the so-called youth soccer industrial complex. I have played on both ends of the spectrum whether that be Rec soccer on muddy little fields or against the top talent in the US. Based on my experiences, I share the three most important pieces to soccer parenting.

1. *Don't yell; this can be applied to all youth sports, It seems so simple, yet is disregarded in every game. Yelling does not help. Yelling at the referee will not change his decision. Yelling at your kid won't help him play better. Yelling at the other team won't make them play worse. In every game I have ever played there has always been that one parent who won't shut up. Your role at your kid's soccer game is not to coach, motivate, or change the game. Your role is to enjoy, observe, and support your kid when they are doing something they like. Now, this is not to say you shouldn't care, you should and will care because you are invested in your child and want them to succeed. But when you yell at the referee, a coach, or a player, it takes away from our experience.*

2. *Make sure that your child enjoys the game of soccer, and not for*

external reasons. I often see players who don't try because they don't want to be out there; it's just not fun for them. They often play because their parents want them to play, or they think they should. Soccer ends up becoming a job for them, which is not what the sport should be. Ask yourself, is my child playing soccer because I want them to? Or ask your child why they are playing soccer. If there isn't any enjoyment for them, then there is no point to it.

3. *The best gift you can give to your child is honesty in an age where everyone gets participation trophies and everyone is told they did a great job regardless of how they actually played. If they played a great game let them know. Be specific about what they did that was so great.*
If your child did not have a great game, then you have to let them know but in a way that is still supportive. If you tell them they had a great game regardless of how they played, in future situations, they won't know whether to trust you or not. Your child won't know what a great performance is from a mediocre one because you told them they were great either way. It will not help them play at higher levels. Your advice will only help them if you are honest. It means so much more to me when I have a great game and my parents tell me that I played a great game because I know that they are honest with me. If I had a bad game they would not be shy to tell me I was off that day. But it only made me better. It only made it sweeter when I played amazing and they let me know I played amazing.

I believe you and your child will have an excellent time in the world of soccer if you ensure that your child really enjoys soccer, you are honest and you ARE NOT YELLING. Good luck.

Eli M.
17-year-old soccer player

Letter from Younger Youth Player to Soccer Parents

Dear Parent,

Here is some advice from a teenage girl soccer player... Never pressure your kid to play a sport or encourage them to move up if they don't want to. It's about enjoying the game. If your kid wants to move to a higher level or get more serious in the game, let them make the change to get better. Don't make them go out to the field to train. When you pressure your kid to do something it makes them want to do it less. You were a kid once. Self-motivation is the most important thing for us to succeed in our goals.

Do not yell at your kid on the field or at anyone else during games. We will either ignore it, get frustrated with you which will likely mess up our game or we will be disappointed in ourselves and feel we aren't good enough. We will most likely have a much worse game than if you aren't yelling at us. We will probably talk about you on the bench. Snarky comments, being disappointed, or treating your kid differently after a bad game is the wrong way to go. Winning is so nice, but, in reality, winning is not important. It's always disappointing when you lose, but it's not important. Losing a game is a learning experience for us so do not make us feel bad for it or make it sound like it's our fault. We play a team game, so we win and lose as a team and work on getting better together.

Remember we play a physical sport so getting injured is a common reality in our lives. Before you say something like "really another injury?" assess the situation of how we are feeling before you make a snarky comment because it will get into our heads.

Parents yelling at the ref is so unnecessary. Refs do not always make good calls, but you yelling at them is going to do absolutely nothing but irritate the ref which does not work to our advantage. It's part of the game.

Don't go to your kid's game if you're going to sit on your phone instead of watching. It makes us feel very unappreciated or like you don't care about what we are passionate about.

And thanks for driving us to soccer...

Alexi M.
13-year-old player

Interview with an Entry-Level Player for Soccer Parents

Scott: What are some of your favorite things to do?

Sammy: Play Mario Party (only 30 minutes every few days, I promise), soccer, wrestle with Joe (little brother) and Daddy...and ninja class.

Scott: Why do you like ninja class?

Sammy: Because I learn how to be a ninja.

Scott: What do you like about the class?

Sammy: There are other boys in it.

Scott: What are some of the things you really like about soccer?

Sammy: Kicking the ball and there are lots of my favorite players.

Scott: So you like watching soccer?

Sammy: Sometimes.

Scott: What are some of your favorite things about playing soccer?

Sammy: It's fun to be on a team with someone, like when we're playing with Ollie and Rhett (his cousins).

Scott: Is there anything else you like about soccer?

Sammy: Watching games with you…and I like to help coach too.

Scott: That's right! Why do you like helping me coach?

Sammy: I like to put the balls and cones on the field.

Scott: Is it that you like coaching or that you like helping me?

Sammy: I like helping you.

Longform Summary

As you read the letters, three points should standout. First, successful youth soccer players, much like successful adults, are internally motivated. If you don't see that motivation in your child's involvement with the game, it might be time to sit down and discuss other athletic or artistic options. One of the best things we can do for our kid's futures is to allow them to find success through their own internal drive. Maybe that comes from playing soccer, maybe not, and that's okay.

Secondly, as our two youth players, and virtually all their peers, are begging is that we stop yelling at them and the referees. Yelling is a distraction and anxiety-builder, not a pressure release valve that clears the way for peak performance. The players' minds are full of game-related thoughts. If improved performance is what we desire, we have to let them work in peace.

Finally, we hope you saw the role of community and relationships in developing a love for the game. Establishing relationships within a team and encountering adversity through the game in a social setting is such a powerful tool for these young people. These experiences have a transformational impact on the kids, be it positive or negative.

If we, as parents, take a holistic view of sports, we'll see them as opportunities for soccer, character, and social development. Our kids will come away with a better grasp of conflict resolution and advocating for themselves. They'll lay the foundation for positive physical habits. Linking internal motivation to passions and opportunities will become the norm.

Ultimately, development won't simply revolve around soccer. Instead, our kids will learn to analyze their actions and environments to find developmental opportunities across all areas of life. We'll take that win over a plastic U12 trophy any day.

What we're doing is, first of all, the focus isn't even really on the kid. The focus is on the parent and getting a parent to understand what development looks like. What role can a parent play in facilitating a love for the ball?... Like a kid in Brazil, Neymar, for example, doesn't fall in love with playing soccer. He falls in love with the ball first...and don't take it from me. Those were Neymar's father's words.

This is much more about parenting, showing and also giving the opportunity to a parent to interact more with

their child where they normally wouldn't. It really is focused on the parent and I call it the 'gift now'. I rephrase it and I say that the gift to the parents is the parents understanding of their child's need for parental attention, parental approval, and parental praise. That's it.

If you figure that out, what happens is that interaction between child and parent creates an electrical, chemical reaction in the child, which is emotions. When you can create an emotionally charged environment, that's where deep learning and long-term memory take place.

So I am convinced that the countries that develop the best players in the world, the number one thing that they get right is they win the battle at the entry-level. Full stop. They win the battle at the entry-level. They're not doing anything different in the way of coaches' education, curriculums, elite player pathways, better facilities…no way. And if they did, if those were all the major ingredients, then America would be winning the World Cup every four years because we've got the best facilities in the world and we've got many more, but we lose the battle at the entry-level. So what happens is that everybody believes the battle is at the elite level because they've lost the entry-level. They don't even understand that.

-Tom Byer

SECTION TWO:
Learning about the Game

Key Terms

If you've ever heard a phrase or word at a soccer game and reacted with a blank stare, think of this section as your field guide.

Below are terms for parents who are new to the sport, as well as those with advanced knowledge. You might even catch the coach off-guard with some of these terms.

While it's not an exhaustive list, it's more than enough to help you see, describe, and converse about many aspects of the game. We believe it's incredibly important to learn about the sports your child plays. The more you know, the better you can guide them in their developmental process and enjoy their play. As a bonus, if you show a willingness to learn, both in general and about your child's interests, they'll see the importance of a daily commitment to intellectual development.

Don't feel you need to memorize all these terms, but do think of this section as a quick game day reference.

People on the Field

Defenders/Backs

The last line of the team's formation is situated between the midfielders and goalkeeper. Centerbacks are often the deepest field players while the outside-backs roam higher up the field. You may hear terms like "stopper" and "sweeper" as well, but those roles are relics of past formations.

Forwards/Striker

The highest line of the formation, these players will account for the majority of the team's goals. "Forwards" describes the whole line whereas "striker" is specific to the central forward.

Goalkeeper/Goalie/Keeper/Keep
The only players allowed to use their hands within their own penalty box. They are the shot-stoppers and critical players in attacking build-ups.

Midfielders/Mids

The link between the defenders and forwards. They epitomize the two-way nature of the game and generally control the flow of the match.

Referee/Ref and Assistant Referee/Linesman

More on this group and their specific roles later, but they are the people who enforce the Laws of the Game and protect the players. The referee is the central figure, whereas the assistant referees, or linesmen, patrol the sidelines.

Wingers

Players who operate primarily in the wings, typically either as a forward or midfielder. Some formations call for wing-backs, which are defenders who primarily occupy the team's wings and are more attack-oriented.

Field of Play

Corner Arc

Arc at the four corners of the pitch where corner kicks are taken.

Defensive Third/Middle Third/Attacking Third

Cut the field into thirds, then start with the third your team is defending. That's the defensive third, the middle third is self-explanatory, and the attacking third features the goal you're attacking. The thirds are relative to each team, so one team's defensive third is the other's attacking third.

Endline/Goal line

The lines on the ends of the field where the goals are situated.

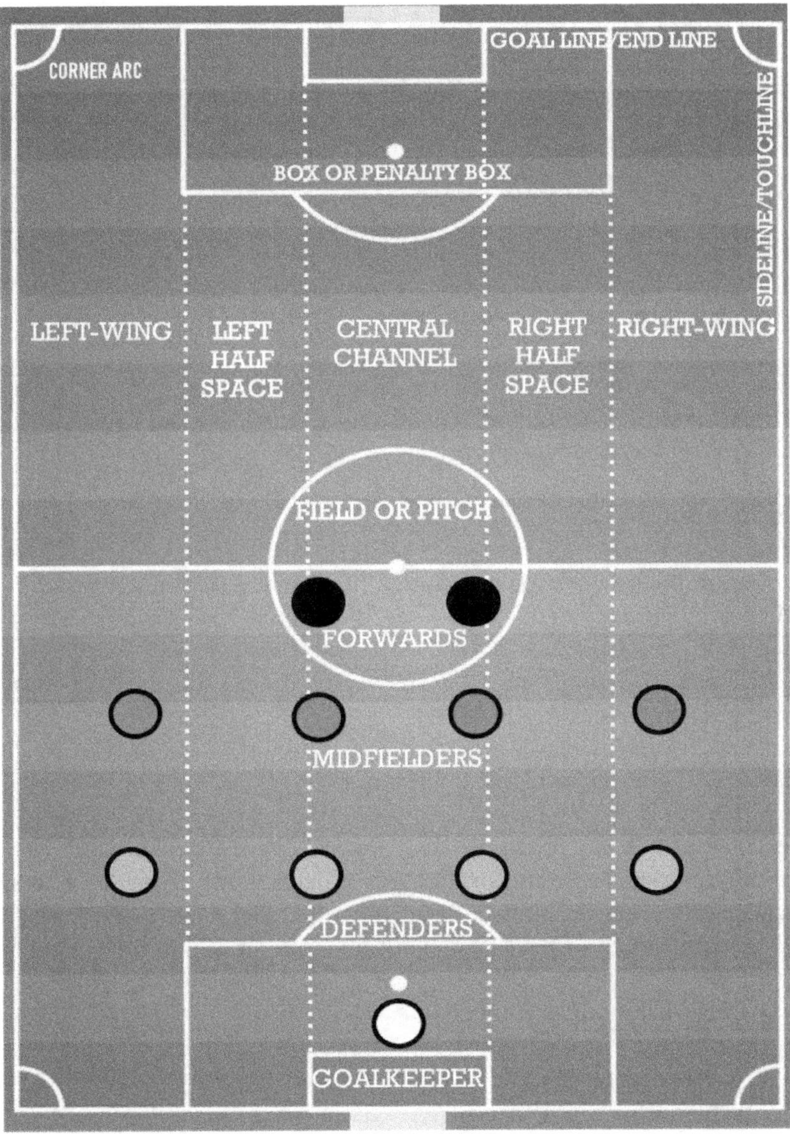

Far post vs Near Post

Terms relative to the positioning of the ball. The far post is the one that's further from the ball while the near post is nearer.

Pitch

Another name for the field. We'll use "pitch" often.

Penalty Area/Box/18
The rectangular box in which the goalie can use his hands. If fouls are committed here, a penalty kick is awarded.

Penalty Spot

The circle in the penalty area designated for penalty kicks. Full-size fields measure the spot at 12 yards from goal, but that distance is shorter for younger age groups.

Sidelines/Touchline

Lines on the side of the pitch. Keep the name "touchline" in mind.
The 6

The small rectangle inside the penalty area. Goal kicks must be taken from within the 6.

Wings/Half Space/Central Channel

Breakdown of the pitch into five vertical channels. The wings, left and right, range from the sideline to the penalty box. The half spaces, again with a left and a right, span from the edge of the 18 to the 6. Finally, the width of the 6 marks out the central channel.

Attacking Lingo

1st/2nd/3rd Attackers

1st Attacker has possession of the ball, 2nd attacker is the immediate support player who's directly involved in the play, and the 3rd attacker is indirectly involved.

1v1

A dribbling scenario pitting one player against another. Take note of specific encounters. If there's space behind the defender that the attacker can dribble into, only then do we have a true 1v1 battle.

3rd Man Run

Remember that 3rd attacker? A 3rd man run is when the 3rd attacker makes an aggressive, up-field run off the ball while the 1st and 2nd attackers connect passes.

Chop/Cut

When an attacker engages a defender, the most common dribbling moves you'll see are lateral and diagonal chops and cuts, either with the inside or outside of the foot.

Counterattack

A quick and direct attack against a vulnerable defense.

Cross

A pass into the box from the wider regions of the field. Crosses can come early (higher up the pitch), cut backs from the end line, target either post, or originate from the half spaces.

Dummy

Intentionally letting the ball run between the legs so that it continues on to a teammate. Think of an intentional nutmeg.

Feint

Another word for a fake, common with dribbling moves.

Final Ball

The pass that leads to an attack on goal. Think of it as a transition from "attacking the opponents" to "attacking the goal."

Finish

A shot from close range that prioritizes placement over power.

First touch/Directional touch

First touch is self-explanatory, but it's important to remember that, if a second touch is desired, first touches are often best when taken either in the direction of the next action or as a means of deceiving the opponent. That's opposed to stopping the ball directly under foot.

Give-and-Go/Wall-Pass
A passes to B, who passes back to A.

Hospital Ball

A poorly hit pass that endangers a teammate by inviting a strong challenge from an opponent, such as a studs-up tackle.

Inswinger vs Outswinger

Crosses that swing in towards the goal or out away from it.

Man On

A common saying to communicate pressure from a defender.

Nutmeg

Sliding the ball between an opponent's legs.

Off the Ball Movement

Movements off the ball to manipulate an opponent's defensive shape or the act of claiming space that is beneficial.

Outlets

Teammates positioned outside of the opponent's pressure who are offering passing options.

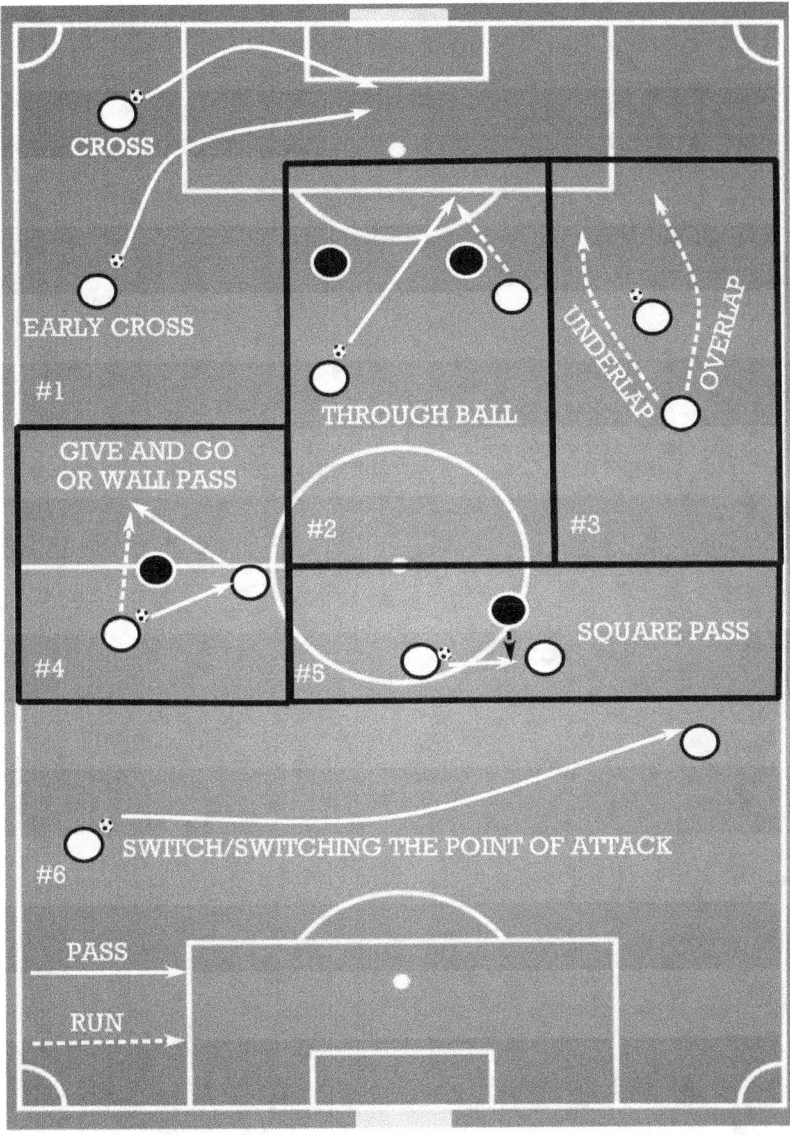

Overlap/Underlap

An overlap is a run around a teammate into a wider area. Underlaps are runs around a teammate into a more central part of the pitch.

Penetrate

Breaking the opponent's defensive press/structure.

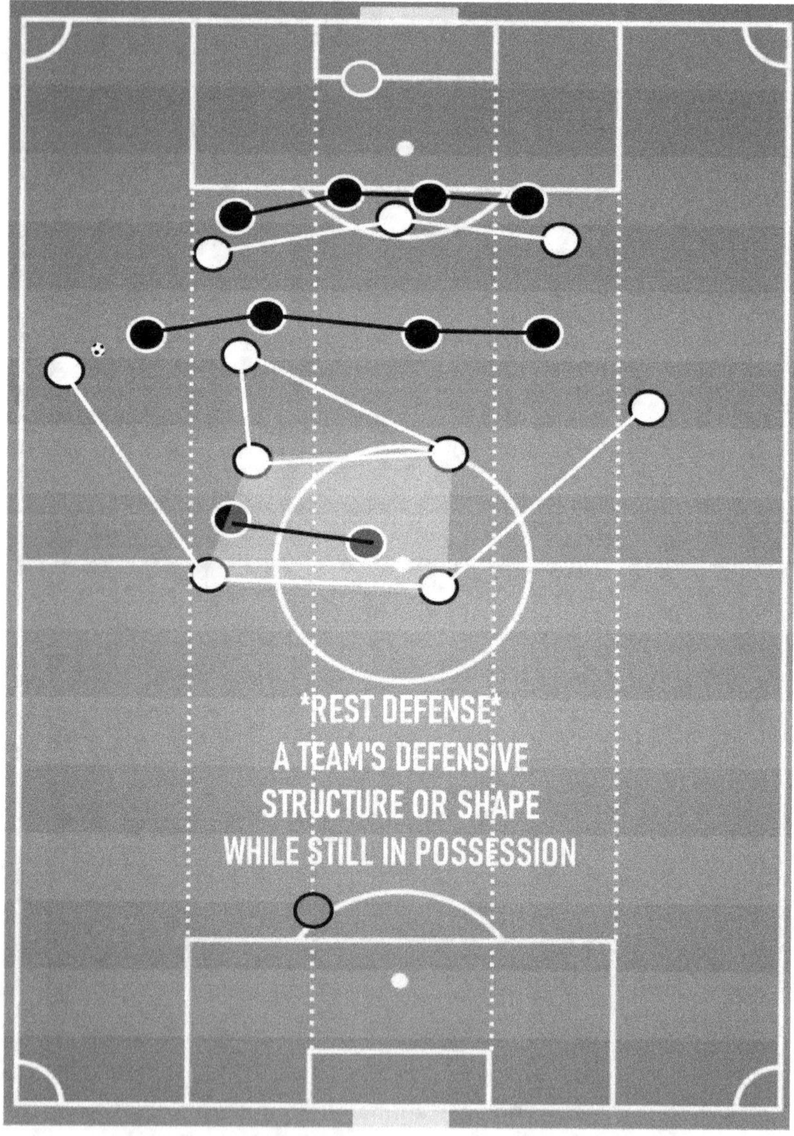

Rest Defense

Rest defense is a team's structure while they're still in possession. A strong rest defense allows teams to limit the opposition's counterattacking opportunities.

Shielding

Using one's body to protect the ball from the opponent's tackle.

Side On

Orienting one's body so that the player's back faces one of the two sidelines to maximize the angle of the field a player can see at any given time.

Square vs Diagonal

Square passes are lateral, diagonal, well, you get it. Diagonal passes are often safest and most dangerous because they move the opponent horizontal and vertical axes. Square are often dangerous because, if the ball is stolen, the defender has already bypassed two opponents.

Switching play/Switching the Point of Attack

Moving the ball from one wing to the other. The general principle is to build up in one area to create space in another. Switching play into the largely unoccupied far side of the field is a great example of this concept.

Through Ball

A pass that is sent through the gap between two opponents, sending a teammate behind the opposition's defensive line.

Time

As opposed to "man on," calling out "time" tells your teammate there's no immediate threat forcing them to release the ball.

Defensive Actions

Ball-side

Positioning oneself between the ball and the opponent you're marking. This helps to take away the passing lane.

Close Down

Reduce the space between you and the opponent.

Defensive Stance

1) Feet in an "L" shape with the front foot pointing at the ball (to either poke tackle or push off to run with the opponent). 2) Knees slightly bent, 3) feet shoulder-width apart, 4) chest over the front knee, and 5) arms slightly out for balance and to initiate contact.

First Contact Point

In 1v1 duels, initiate a high first contact point, using the hands, wrists, or forearms to slow the opponent and establish positioning. Mind you, full arm extension is a foul, but these high points of first contact are generally legal if the elbow remains bend. Basic principle: go high instead of low in most tackles to keep balance and power through the contact.

Goal-Side

Positioning oneself between the goal and the opponent you're marking. This helps to contest passes played into the space behind the backline.

Guard/Mark

Taking responsibility for a nearby opponent.

Interception

To win possession of an opponent's pass.

Pressure/Cover/Balance

Remember 1st/2nd/3rd attackers? Same thing on the defensive side of the ball. The 1st defender is the "pressure defender," meaning they're the player directly engaged with the opponent on the ball. "Cover defenders" are the 2nd defenders, offering protection to the first defender. If the pressure defender is beat, a cover defender transitions into a first defender role. Balance refers to the remaining players in the team's defensive structure. Note that with cover defenders, more than one player can offer coverage.

Recover and Backtrack

A recovery run, or backtracking, is the run from an attacking position high up the field back into the team's deeper defensive shape.

Stab

Don't encourage stabbing Lunging forward with one foot in an attempt to tackle the ball. Transferring weight to the front foot leaves the defender off-balance and unable to further contest the attacker. The attempt at a low point of first contact sacrifices balance in the defensive stance, making it an easy approach to beat.

Tackle - Block, Side Block, Poke, Slide

Block tackles use the foot to block the forward path of the ball. A *side block tackle* funnels the opponent to one side before using the hips and shoulder to block their path to the ball. Shoulder and hip charges/contact offer physical resistance in side block challenges. *Poke tackles* look similar to a stab, but balance is maintained throughout the tackle. Rather than transferring weight to the front foot, a player's balance remains on the back foot while the front foot quickly pokes forward at the ball before returning to a balanced defensive stance. It's the best tackle to use when an opponent tries to cut across the defender's body. *Slide tackles* involve sliding on the ground to cover greater distance in the tackle, typically out of desperation.

Wall

In set piece situations, walls involve players lining up side-by-side to limit the shooter's ease and angles to goal.

Ball Striking

Bend

The curveball version of soccer. A right-footed bent pass or shot moves significantly to the right before BENDing back to the left.

Bicycle Kick

With their back to goal, a player leaps into the air with their back parallel to the ground, striking the ball above their head.

Chip

A gently lofted pass with almost no follow-through. Not a driven ball. Instead, it will seem to float through the air.

Drive

A strike to maximize distance, which you'll often see from goalkeepers during goal kicks.

Header

Striking the ball with the forehead, just at the hairline. One-footed jumps are used from running starts, two-footed jumps from a standstill.

Ping

A low, driven ball with backspin. The downward, diagonal striking motion applies the backspin, slowing the pace of the ball in flight before reducing speed further upon contact with the ground. It's a great technique for through balls to keep the ball from rolling to the goalkeeper.

Punt

A goalkeeper's kick that starts with the ball in hands before dropping to the swinging foot.

Trivela

Same concept as the bend, but with the outside of the foot.

Volley

Striking the ball while it's still in flight. The half volley variation is when the ball bounces off the ground before the player hits it while it's still in the air.

Game Actions

Advantage

When a fouling offense is committed, but the possessing team still holds an attacking advantage. If a foul looks like it should have been given, but play continues, this is typically the reason.

Assist

The pass leading to a goal.

Brace

When a player scores two goals in a game.

Corner Kick

A direct free kick taken from the corner arc.

Extra Time

Also known as injury or stoppage time, it's additional time added to a game to account for injuries and other stoppages. Extra time in a tournament format encompasses overtime.

Set Piece

A restart from a dead ball/static situation. Set pieces are the free-kick variants that lead to attacks on goal.

Goal

When the ball crosses entirely over the goal line, within the frame of the goalposts, which is worth one point.

Goal Kick

A free kick given when one team puts the ball out of bounds over the opponent's endline. The kick is taken from inside the 6-yard box.

Halftime

A five to 15-minute break (depending on the level of play) between the two halves of play.

Hat Trick

When a player scores three goals in a game.

Key Pass

A pass that leads to a shot.

Own Goal

Scoring a goal against your own team.

Play On

A common shout from the referee when he allows the attacking team to play an advantage (see above) rather than whistling for a foul.

Tactical Terminology

Blocks and Press - Low, Middle, High

A "low block" is when a team defends in their defensive third, whereas a "middle block" is when the team's defensive structure is predominantly in the middle third of the pitch. The "high press" when a team is actively defending in the attacking/final third.

Between the lines

When a player position's himself "between the lines" of the opposition's formations, such as between defenders and midfielders.

Formation

A set of lines and general positional references that allow a team to carry out their philosophy.

Line of Confrontation vs Line of Resistance

A line of confrontation is the place where a team starts pressing the opponent. If midfield is the line of confrontation, the highest players in the formation will drop to midfield before actively pressuring the opposition. Structure over immediate pressure.

The line of resistance is how deep the lowest-positioned field players are positioned. If the defenders are positioned at the top of the box (top of the 18), then that's the line of resistance.

Overload and Unbalance

An overload is committing additional players to the ball, so it's primarily a quantitative measure. While it makes space near the ball a little tighter, the objective is generally to create more space elsewhere.

That happens once the opponent are "unbalanced" near the ball. By unbalanced, we mean the third/balance defenders (see Pressure/Cover/Balance) have overcommitted near the ball in an effort to recover it, leaving them vulnerable and out of position elsewhere.

Style of Play/Philosophy

An overarching set of principles by which a team approaches the game.

Superiorities - 4 types

Quantitative – A numerical advantage.

Qualitative – Possessing greater quality in a specific area than the opponent.

Positional – Owning better positional structure to achieve a tactical objective. Highly specific and tough to pick out for beginner and intermediate viewers.

Socio-Affective – A "sum is greater than their parts" type of superiority. It's the connection of a group of players with an incredible understanding of how to play with each other and play against the opponent.

Tactics

The specific actions within the style of play/philosophy that are tailored to a specific opponent. The contrast between tactics and philosophy is one of specific vs general.

Common (Random) Soccer Terms

Jersey/Kit

The uniform players wear at games.

Juggle

Keeping the ball off the ground, much like juggling with hands, but without the use of hands or arms.

Promotion and relegation

If a team is promoted, that means they're advancing to a higher division or competition. Relegation is the inverse, moving down a level.

Rondo

Keep away games with various setups. Great for training decision making, spatial and temporal awareness, technique, body orientation, and deception.

Naughty List Words (Eliminate These)

Boot it!

Booting the ball is a purposeless kick up the field with no thought other than the hope that my teammate gets to the ball before the opponent does. A team that uses non-stop booting is called "kick-and-run," showing the lack of intelligence and purpose in their game. Kick-an-run teams play big, dumb, and ugly...and often receive false feedback at the younger or less skilled ages through wins and goals. If you want development, demand more. Start by eliminating "boot it" from the sidelines.

Do (fill in the blank)!

Telling a player what to do strips them of a valuable learning experience. It also takes away the in-game feedback that coaches need in order to properly assess their teams. Cheer, but don't direct (more on that distinction later).

Kick it!

Much like "boot it," saying "kick it" conveys an imprecise action. I want my players to pass the ball, maybe ping or bend it to "X". Those terms convey a purpose. "Kick it" does not.

Summary

1. Don't get too caught up on the key terms. If some of the descriptions have helped you clear up some confusion and helped you understand some common sayings, that's

enough.

2. The list is extensive, but not exhaustive. If you hear a new phrase or term, don't be afraid to ask about it.

3. The images should help visualize a number of the terms, but remember that tutorials for most of the technical actions can be found on YouTube.

The Laws of the Game

Referee, assistant referee, and what's VAR?

The referee controls the match, enforcing the Laws of the Game and ensuring the protection of the players. Additionally, central refs keep match records and serve as the timekeeper.

Assistant referees help the referee by monitoring when the ball leaves the field of play, then providing instructions for re-entry. They're also responsible for tracking offsides and facilitating substitutions.

At higher levels of play, typically top-level professionals, you might see a 4th official or the use of VAR (Video Assistant Referee). 4th officials track wasted time and take over substitution procedures. VAR checks for penalty kick and red card offenses.

Offsides

Watching the professional game, offsides may seem like one of the two most difficult rules to understand, the other being what constitutes a handball. VAR should make the rule more clear, but it typically leads to greater disagreement. Application is more of an issue than what's written, especially when the Video Assistant Referee is not involved.

The simplified version is that an attacking player cannot actively take part in the play if there aren't two opponents between him and the goal, but only in the attacking half of the field. One of those opponents is typically a goalie, the other is often a defender.

The attacking player is allowed to stand in an offside position, but he cannot immediately participate in the play. For example, if a player is standing in the space between the goalie and the deeper of two centerbacks, he is in an offside position, but, since he's not yet engaged in the play, there is no offense. If the pass is played to him while he's behind the deepest defender, then the whistle is blown and an indirect kick (more on this in a moment) is given to the defending team.

Offsides is also called when the player in an offside position interferes with play. This doesn't happen often, but the most common occurrences involve screening the goalkeeper or a defender. While not "active" in the play, the attacker is interfering with an active opponent, limiting their participation.

Now, let's look at an example where the player, Tom, starts offside but is not actively involved in the initial play. Say a teammate, Francisco, who was in an onside position, received the ball and dribbled past his defender. He's not only beat his opponent, but Francisco dribbled beyond everyone, including Tom, and now has a breakaway to goal. While Francisco dribbles to goal, Tom runs down the field, a few steps behind Francisco. As Francisco enters the box, the goalie comes out to meet him to cut down the shooting angle. Rather than shooting, Francisco passes the ball to Tom, who was a couple of steps behind his teammate. Tom has a better angle to goal and calmly scores. A goal is given.

But why?

Even though Tom was initially in an offside position, he was not directly involved in Francisco's 1v1 duel and breakaway. As Francisco dribbles past his teammate, Tom enters an onside position because he's behind the ball. Even though two opponents aren't between Tom and the goal, the ball is. That condition resets Tom's positioning, meaning he's now onside.

So, to summarize, either two opponents OR the ball must be between the attacker and the goal. Just remember those conditions only apply in the attacking half of the field. Offsides does not apply in the defensive half or during goal kicks, corner kicks, and throw-ins.

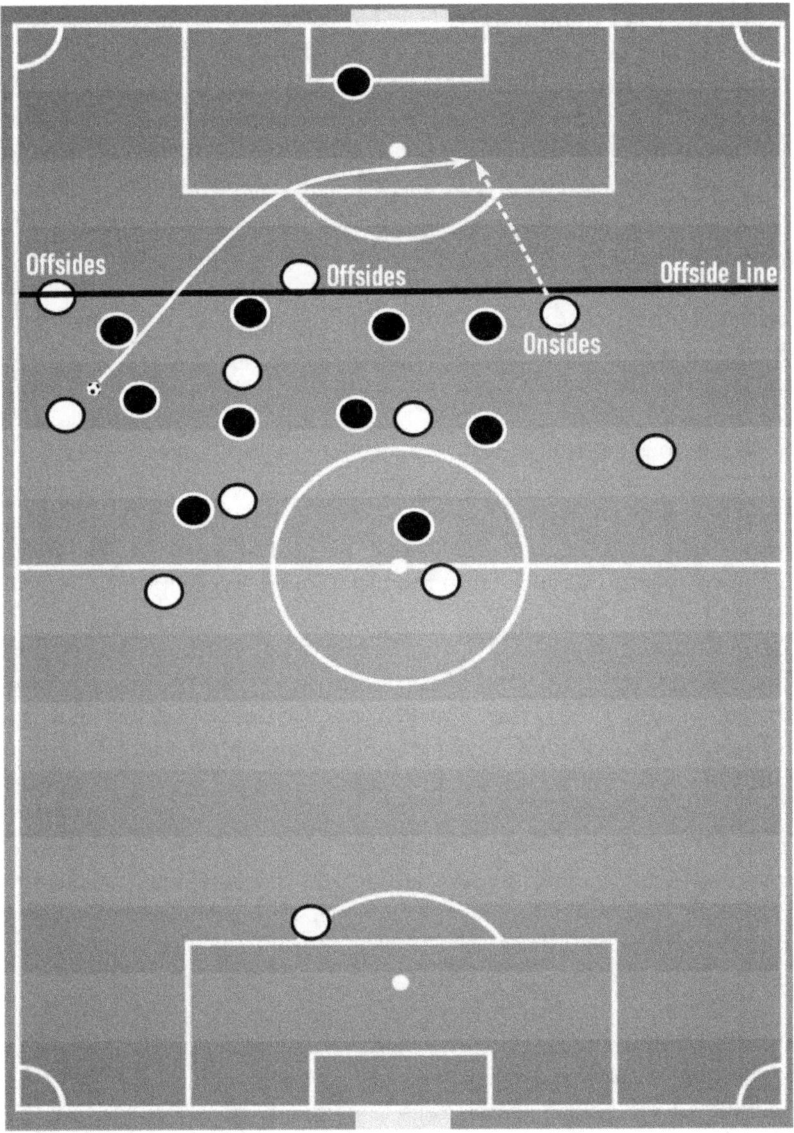

Offsides
Offsides
Offside Line
Onsides

Handling (aka handball)

If you thought offsides was a convoluted rule, you're in luck...handling, also called handball, is even more confusing.

It's not so much that the rule itself is confusing, but the subjective application will lead to some head-scratching moments, even for the most experienced coaches, players, and fans. VAR's role in reviewing handling situations in the box led to a 38% increase in penalty kicks from the 2018/19 season to 2019/20 in the Italian top division, Serie A. But, at the youth level, we don't have the benefit of VAR, so all calls are subject to the referee's immediate view of the play.

So, what does the rule state?

Handling is when the ball hits the hand or arm, except the upper arm, which falls in line with the lowest part of the armpit. Basically, handling requires a touch from the bicep to the fingertips.

After listing the rule, IFAB, the International Football Association Board that creates the Laws of the Game, then lists 12 conditions for the rule. We won't go through them one-by-one, but know that the full-length Laws of the Game are available through the IFAB website and app.

To briefly summarize the 12 conditions, know that there either has to be some level of intent to handle the ball or a significant advantage gained by that contact, even if incidental. If in a game, Ava takes a shot that glances off of Maria's hand and into the goal, a handling call is appropriate even though Maria didn't intend for the contact.

Another important aspect is the positioning of the arms. Say Maria is looking to switch the point of attack to her right. Lilly is there, waiting for the ball. As Maria tries to chip the ball in her teammate's direction, the ball strikes an opponent's outstretched arm. While the opponent didn't intend to handle the ball, her outstretched arm was away from the rest of her body, which is what IFAB terms as making "their body unnaturally bigger."

Even in the "unnaturally bigger" qualification, distance is an important factor. Greater distances mean the player has more time to adapt the position of their arms for the incoming contact. From within five yards, you'll often see referees NOT call handling, unless the offense takes place in the penalty box. The rationale is that the player has too little time to adapt to the flight of the ball, especially if the arm is reasonably close to the body.

It's a simple rule in thought, but one of the two most complex in application.

Fouls

Fouls or misconduct cover a broad spectrum but suffice it to say that this is an offense when the ball is in play. In such cases, a direct or indirect free kick is given.

Direct Kicks vs Indirect Kicks

Let's talk about those direct kicks. A general rule of thumb is that direct kicks are given when a play is deemed careless, reckless, or using excessive force.

If one of those three conditions isn't met, an indirect kick is given. For the most part, indirect free kicks are the product of offsides calls or unsporting behavior.

What's the difference between the kicks?

Direct kicks can go directly into the goal. One touch, one goal. Indirect kicks can only enter the goal indirectly, so two touches minimum are necessary. If the referee's arm is raised straight in the air, the kick is indirect. If her arms are by her side, the kick is direct.

Advantage

If an offense occurs but the non-offending team benefits from the continuation of play, referees can allow teams to "play the advantage." If a supposed advantage is immediately lost, referees may also whistle the play dead and award a free kick.

Restarting Play

Kickoff - Used to start each half and restart play after a goal, kickoffs can be played in any direction, including straight back with the first touch, an addendum to the rules in 2016.

Drop Ball - Another recently modified rule (June 2019), a dropped ball is a way of returning play to the team in possession after an emergency halt of play, which includes the ball hitting the referee. If the stoppage takes place with the ball in the penalty box, the play is dropped for the goalkeeper.

For plays stopped outside of the box, the ball is dropped for the team that last had possession. The ball is dropped where it was last touched before the stoppage. One player receives the ball while everyone else must remain at least 4.5 yards (four meters) away.

Goal Kick

When the attacking team puts the ball out of play over the endline, a goal kick is awarded to the defending team.

In the past, goal kicks had to leave the box before play resumed. As of June 2019, the team taking the goal kick has no restrictions. If they want to pass to a teammate who's in the box, they are free to do so.

Also, remember that offsides does not apply to goal kicks.

Corner Kick

Like a goal kick, corner kicks are the result of the ball crossing over the endline. The difference between the two is in which team put the ball out of play.

While goal kicks signal the last touch was off of an attacking player, corner kicks are awarded when the last touch is off of a player from the defending team.

Taken from the corner arch, the offsides law does not apply to corner kicks.

Throw-Ins

Now, for touchline (sideline) stoppages. Throw-in technique requires the thrower to 1) face the field of play, 2) stand on or behind the touchline, and 3) use both hands to throw the ball over his head from back to front. Miss any of the three steps and an illegal throw is whistled and the other team given the chance to throw the ball into play.

Opponents must give a two-yard cushion to the thrower. If not, they risk a yellow card for unsporting behavior. If the throw-in was already taken, an indirect kick is awarded.

Other offenses include the thrower being the first to touch the ball after the throw. That scenario produces an indirect kick.

Stoppage Time

At the end of each half, the referee is allowed to add minutes to account for stoppages. Among the more common cases are medical stoppages, goal celebrations, disciplinary action, and substitutions.

Professional games add another layer. VAR checks for time-wasting, plus extreme heat hydration breaks also contribute to lost time.

Penalty Kicks

When direct free kick offenses take place in the box, a penalty kick is awarded. Since it is a direct kick, a goal may be scored directly from it.

Setting up the kick, the ball is placed on the penalty mark located 12 yards from goal. The goalkeeper must keep at least one foot on or behind the goal line until the shot is taken. In the goalkeeper leaves the line before the penalty kick is taken, a yellow card can be given, then the kick is retaken.

If the shooter scores and none of his teammates enter the box, we have a goal.

If a player does infringe, be it the goalie, shooter, or another player, there's a range of possible outcomes. Law 14 lists all possibilities, but know that if a kick is retaken or an indirect kick awarded, either someone moved too early or the shooter made a mistake, like an illegal stopping motion or backward pass.

Cards

Yellow - Given for more hostile fouls or foul accumulation, usually four or five, yellow cards serve as a warning. Players on yellow cards must tread carefully because two yellows make one red.

Red - Whether due to a second yellow card or an especially vicious foul, a red card means the offending player is out of the game and his team must play the remaining time with one fewer player on the pitch. Red cards carry a minimum one-game suspension too, though some have ranged for months due to the severity of the foul.

IFAB App

As mentioned, IFAB, the body that determines and creates the Laws of the Game, has a website and app. We highly recommend downloading the app. If a question comes up during a game, you have a great resource available at the tap of a button.

Summary

1. Offside and handling are convoluted rules. Don't worry, they mystify us as well.
2. Most free kicks will be direct with the ref indicating possession by pointing in the direction of the guilty team/direction the possessing team will attack.
3. Download the IFAB app for a helpful, sideline resource.

Understanding Referees

At the core, a referee's job is to enforce the laws of the game. The laws are concrete, but the implementation of the laws is subjective, with each referee having their own styles and imperfections. That's a difficult reality for most coaches, players, and parents to accept. It's in our nature to want some control over matters in our lives.

It's that locus of control that seems to cause the most conflict with referees. They're often viewed as distant, cold, and biased officiators of the game. We tend to look at the calls, or non-calls, that go against our team, especially if it's our own child on the wrong end, and look for fault in the referee's decision. As mentioned, the implementation of the rules is subjective, so we form opinions as to how the rules should be enforced too.

There is a time for the players and coaches to advocate for their team, but, in general, the culture surrounding the treatment of referees is an area that needs to change.

Keeping Emotions in Check

It's tough to see your child in pain because of a hit they've taken. No one enjoys the experience of losing a game because of a call from the referee. Calls, viewed in isolation, always allow for an interpretation of referee bias.

When the game and sideline become heated, it's important to recognize we're becoming too emotionally involved and take a step back. As parents, we do tend to take individual actions, or even a string of poor decisions, personally.

Managing the Game

From the referee's perspective, the objectives are pretty straightforward: 1) enforce the Laws of the Game, 2) protect the players, and 3) manage the game in a predictable manner.

Managing the game is one of the most important aspects of a referee's job. Setting a clear idea of what is acceptable vs unacceptable play influences each player's approach. Let's face it, players want to know where that line is so they can walk it. Sounds a lot like home, doesn't it?

Some of the best referees we've encountered are the ones who take the time to speak to the players during the pregame check-in. They'll have a conversation about the referee's style and let the players know where they draw the line. If a player crosses the line, they have no one to blame but themselves.

That conversation was our greatest tool as referees. Dialogue was open and players acknowledged our approach, which then allowed us to enforce the rules with little argument from the players and coaches. Letting them know that we were physical players ourselves and enjoyed that type of game, we let players know that we would allow for a more physical approach so long as the contact was legal.

For rivalry games, calling the first 10 to 15 minutes a little tighter was another go-to tactic. Though the initial run of play might frustrate the players, it set a clear tone. Easing off as the game progressed and the players adapted to the approach, the results were fantastic. Players enjoyed the freedom but knew they couldn't take it for granted. It's just one approach of many, but it's one that produced a lot of fun matches.

Lessons from the Pitch

You're probably wondering why we've taken the time to walk you through our old reffing styles. In part, it's to give you an idea of the professional and psychological approaches of referees.

Sure, some referees don't like certain clubs or coaches. Maybe a player on the field or parent group has etched a long-term spot in the official's memory too.

Scott's coached one of those players. After a referee warned him about his, well, let's call it, chatter on the field, this young man crossed the line again in the third consecutive game, picking up two quick yellow cards, earning himself a red. It was a short-term annoyance for Scott and his teammates, but hopefully a long-term lesson for this young man.

Even in this scenario, the official was completely within his rights. Having spoken with this specific referee after the first two matches, he made it clear that, if he were to officiate any more of our games, he would confront that player's actions more aggressively. In hindsight, Scott should have followed up on my conversations with the young man with the same rigor as the ref did. More attention to the issue was needed during practices. There was a clear target on his back, but one that he had earned. As his coach, it was Scott's job to work with his parents to guide him through the on-field issues, preferably fixing the problem before the referees intervened.

As parents, we do have a responsibility to view events like the one just described in context. In the vast majority of cases, the referees mean no harm to the individual players or teams. We're not going to like all of their decisions, but the same can be said in nearly any aspect of life. Tell us you've never disagreed with a spouse, boss, friend, or colleague and we'll show you what your bluffing face looks like.

Soccer mimics life. Not all the calls will go your way. A stellar performance doesn't always produce the desired results. Life isn't fair and neither is soccer.

As parents, coaches, and players, we do tend to scapegoat the referees for undesired results. Scott still hasn't forgiven the crew that officiated the 49ers vs Ravens Super Bowl matchup.

In a sense, this is our way of coping with an undesired outcome. It's easier to point the finger at someone else than examine our shortcomings or that of our player/team.

Know that most referees don't come into a game looking to cause issues. Take one minute to Google referee horror stories. From attacks on the field to angry mobs following them to their cars, referees have to deal with the stigma against the profession as well as very real threats against them. Scott will never forget when he, as a 16-year-old ref, was nearly charged by a rec soccer coach who didn't have the slightest grasp of the rules. It was a scary situation. He's used that experience to remind himself that referees are 1) human beings due the respect of their basic human dignity, 2) someone's loved one, and 3) people who love the game and want to stay involved.

Summary

1. As the game becomes emotionally charged, keeping emotions in check helps to keep the physicality of the game from escalating into an uncontrolled state.
2. Referees have three objectives: 1) enforce the Laws of the Game, 2) protect the players, and 3) manage the game in a predictable manner.
3. The vast majority of referees don't come to the field with the urge to cause issues. As parents and coaches, we have to examine our behavior towards officials in light of their humanity, not their position. Object, sure, but never cross the line into violence, verbal abuse, or intimidation.

Positional Roles

Time to move to the fun stuff: player roles and game-specific ideas. We'll start with the player roles, giving an idea of player expectations both in attack and defense.

What goalkeepers do

Starting at the bottom of the field, we have the goalkeepers. The last line of defense, keepers are the only players on the pitch who are allowed to use their hands, which is the reason they must wear a distinct color from their teammates. Off-colored uniforms make it easy for referees to pick out which player is allowed to handle the ball.

So, what else does a goalie do?

Attacking - The modern game requires goalkeepers to use their feet and help their team in the attack. In the early stages, she will often help the team build-out of the back. As the deepest option on the field, her teammates will use her as an outlet for switching the point of attack or drawing the opposition higher up the field, which then creates more space to play into vertically. As the attack progresses, goalies become a deep release valve to relieve pressure and reset the attack.

Defending - For possession dominant teams, it's common to see goalkeepers play well off their line to reduce the space the opponent can attack. Say your goalie is 50 yards behind her defenders. That gives the opponents roughly 20-30 yards to play into. If the goalie reduces that space to 35 yards, she limits the opponent's ability to play behind the defenders. Yes, that does leave the goalie standing outside of her box, but that's fine. Stopping an attack early, high up the pitch with her feet will often save her from facing a 1v1 near her goal.

As opponents move closer to goal, she will command her box, using her positioning to limit the opponent's angle to goal and informing her teammates of the most dangerous threats. Goalkeepers can see the whole field of play, so they're often the loudest, most commanding players on the field, which is a positive.

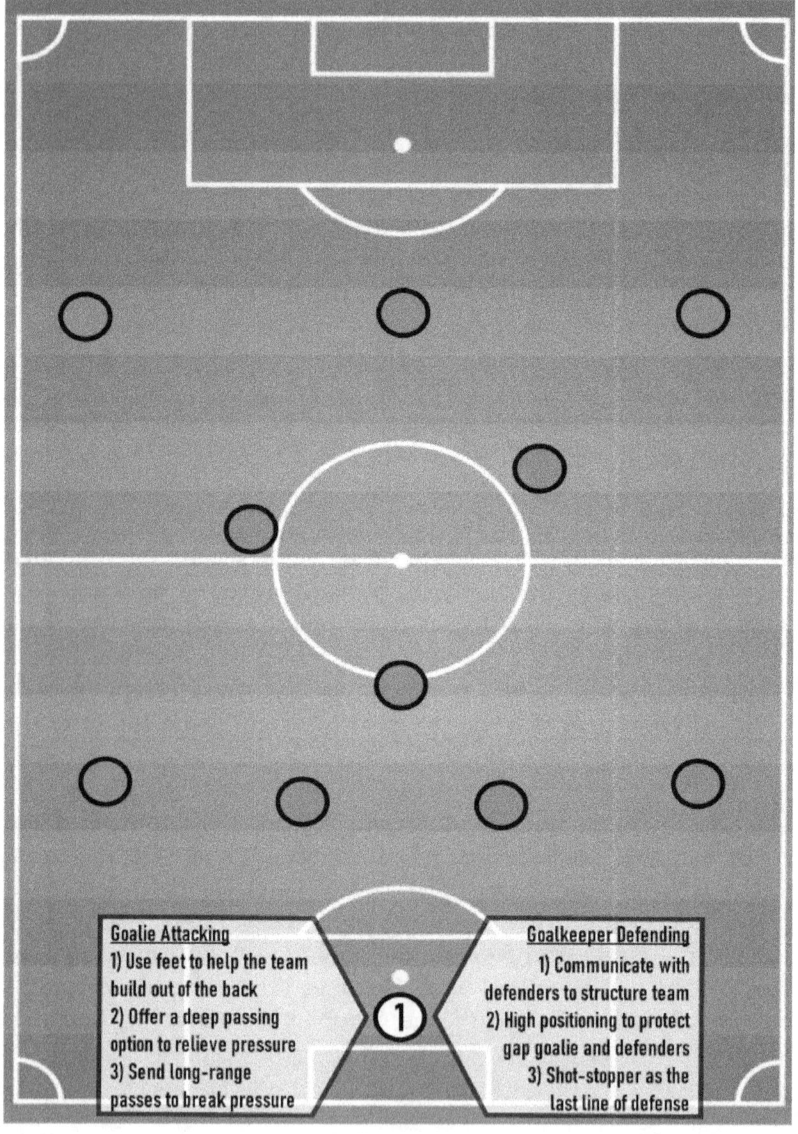

What defenders do

In front of the goalkeeper are the defenders, which, as a unit, are also called the backline. Some teams will play with three centerbacks, others with two flanked by two outside-backs. The distinctions between the center and outside defenders are rather prominent in the modern game, so we'll tackle the descriptions separately.

Centerbacks: *Attacking* - Much like the goalie, centerbacks are often key players as the team builds out of the back. While they don't have to be the most technically gifted players, having the ability to keep possession under pressure, as well as sending intermediate and long-range passes to break the opponent's lines are major distinguishers. In possession dominant teams, centerbacks can offer those long-range passes over defenses in the attacking half of the field too. Finally, they're often tall and strong athletes, meaning they typically take on important roles in set piece situations.

Centerbacks: *Defending* - The last players between the opponent and the goalie, centerback is a high-pressure, high-stakes job. In cooperation with the goalie, centerbacks look to keep the team structured, both in and out of possession. Threat identification and communication are key skills of the position. If the centerbacks don't take away access to the middle of the field or direct the team's structure, goals are coming.

Outside-backs: *Attacking* - In the modern game, outside-backs are primarily wide playmakers. Regardless of a team's formation, outside-backs are often the widest players on the field as their team engages in the attacking half. Dynamic athletes, typically blessed with quickness and speed, these players are best served in larger spaces where they can fully utilize their athleticism.

Outside-backs: *Defending* - When teams successfully integrate outside-backs into the attack, recovery runs and counterpressing are the most important tasks. So, when your team loses the ball, that outside-back who's close to the ball should immediately pressure the opponent to try and recover the ball. If that doesn't work, then a quick retreat into the backline, supporting the centerbacks, is the next step. Outside-backs will drop as deep as necessary to defend, but always have an eye on space to run into when possession is recovered.

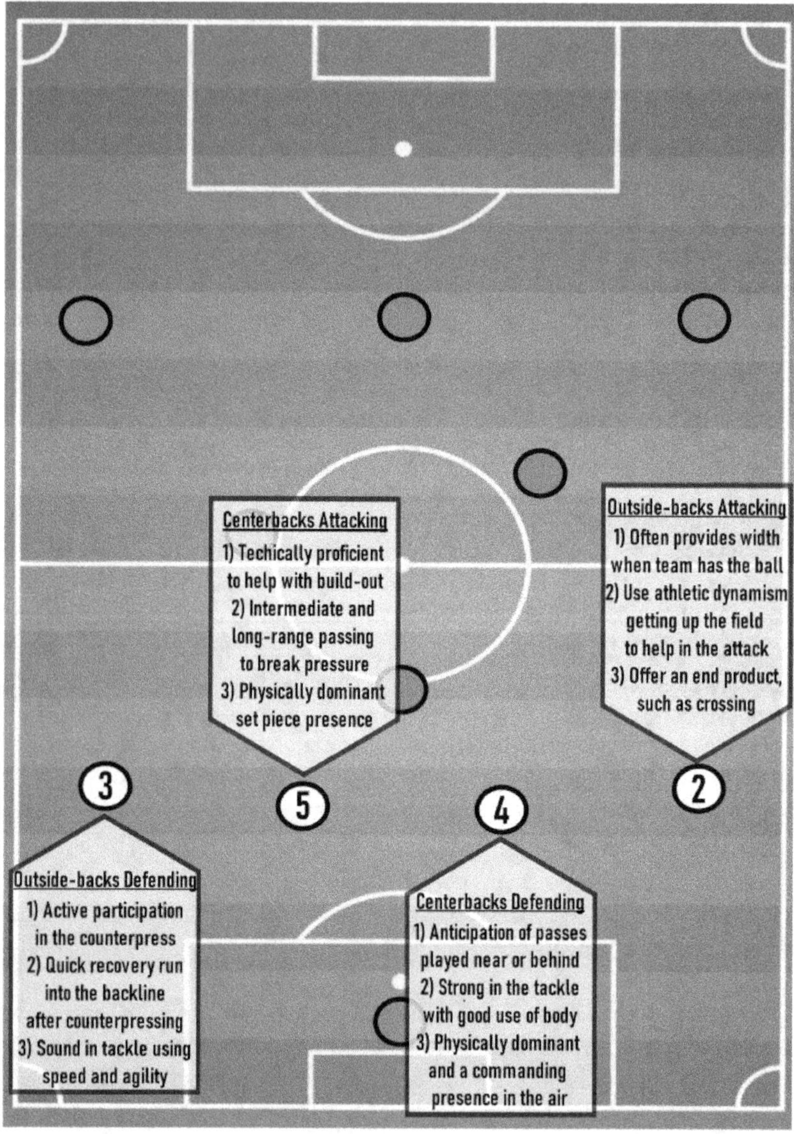

What midfielders do

Much like defenders, there is an outside vs inside dichotomy among midfielders. More athletic, likely less technically gifted players, will take up wider positions while the less athletic, more technically and tactically skilled find central positions.

Defensive midfielders - Usually central players, the #6 protects the backline while also managing the space between the centerbacks and attacking midfielders. Some formations use one while others employ two. The top priority is keeping the opposition from running at the centerbacks. Top defensive qualities include awareness of threats, anticipation of passes into midfield, and technique and physicality in the tackle.

In attack, more tactically skilled and technically proficient defensive mids (tactical #6) can set the tempo of play (how quickly should we move? When do we go? What do we need to accomplish before we engage the opponent?). One of the basic skills is the ability to keep possession with short passes while keeping an eye on longer range, pressure-breaking options.

Box-to-Box midfielders - Much like the name suggests, box-to-box midfielders, or #8, shuttle from one penalty box to the other, playing equal roles in the defensive and attacking halves. Defensively, the #8 must dutifully trackback to help his defensive midfield partner. Picking up runners from midfield is especially important. Contributing to the high press and counterpress are equally important in possession-dominant teams.

In attack, #8s tend to have a Swiss Army knife skill set. They're incredibly versatile and often very intelligent players. They might not be the best athletes or routinely drive the ball to long-range targets, but they're magicians in tight spaces and have fantastic endurance. Cool, collected, intelligent players often excel in this role.

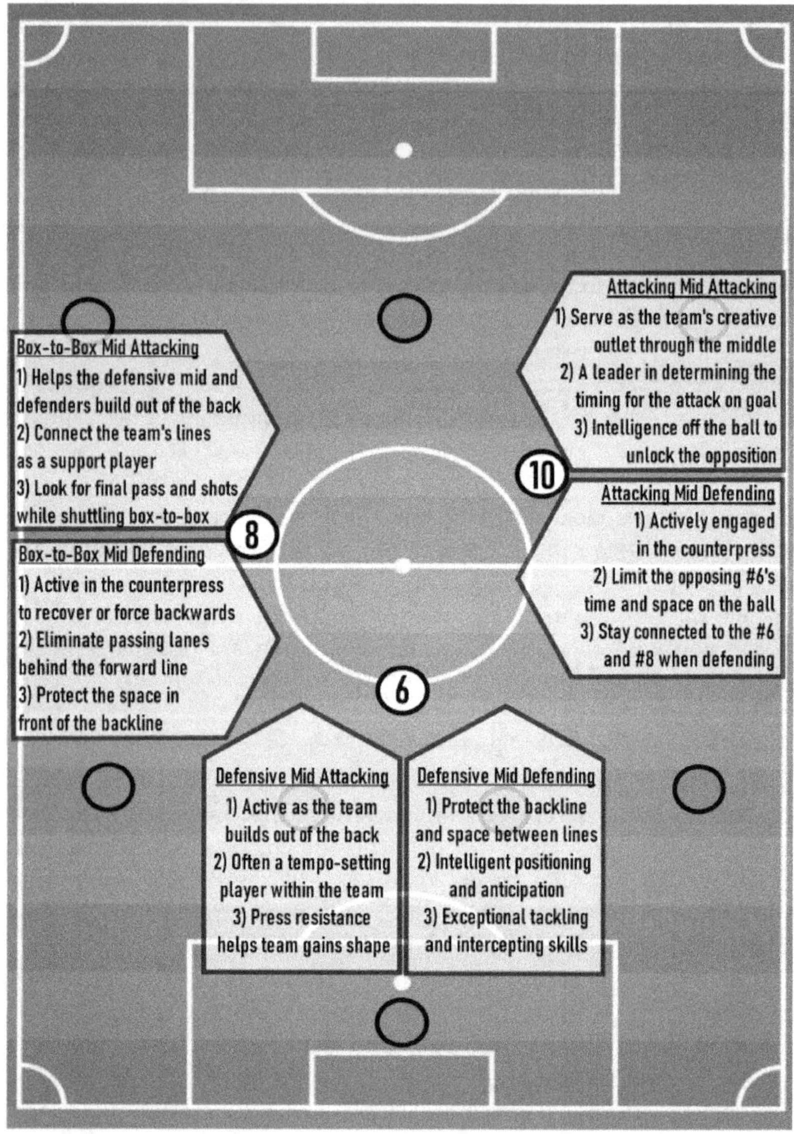

Attacking midfielders - The tactical number for an attacking midfielder is the #10. It's a number associated with many of the greatest attackers and playmakers. Pele, Diego Maradonna, and Lionel Messi all wore the #10 and are arguably three of the top five players to lace up soccer cleats. It's not just a number, but a statement of intent as well. These players are creative, possess dominant technical ability, and have supremely high soccer IQs. They're the "see the play three steps in advance" type of player.

Defensively, #10s must contribute to the high press and counterpress. As play progresses, limiting the opposition's defensive midfielder or dropping in with the #6 and #8 becomes the priority.

An #8/10 hybrid is a more recent development of the role, much like Luka Modrić or Andrés Iniesta, two modern legends of the game. The classic #10 was strictly a creative attacker. Defensive qualities need not apply. However, more holistic pressing structures have required even the most skilled attacking players to contribute to the team's defensive efforts. These days, the attacking burden is still there, but there's a greater emphasis on the defensive side of the game.

Wide Midfielders/Wide Forwards - We're going to cheat and lump wide forwards into this category. The difference between the two is typically down to defensive contributions required by the team's style of play. Less dominant teams will require a greater defensive contribution from the wide midfielders, aka wingers, especially against possession dominant teams.

From an attacking standpoint, the top strengths of wingers tend to be their 1v1 dribbling, recognition and timing of runs, and athleticism. By beating the first defender, they can then throw the opposition's defensive structure totally out of whack. In other words, wingers are wide playmakers with dynamic individual qualities.

What forwards do

Since we've lumped wingers together in the midfield category, we'll focus exclusively on center forwards in this section. Just keep in mind that the 1-4-3-3 formation is very popular at the USA youth levels, so many wingers are better identified as forwards than midfielders. If the winger stays high up the field, often in a wide area, he's signaling that his role within the team's tactics is more closely aligned with that of a forward.

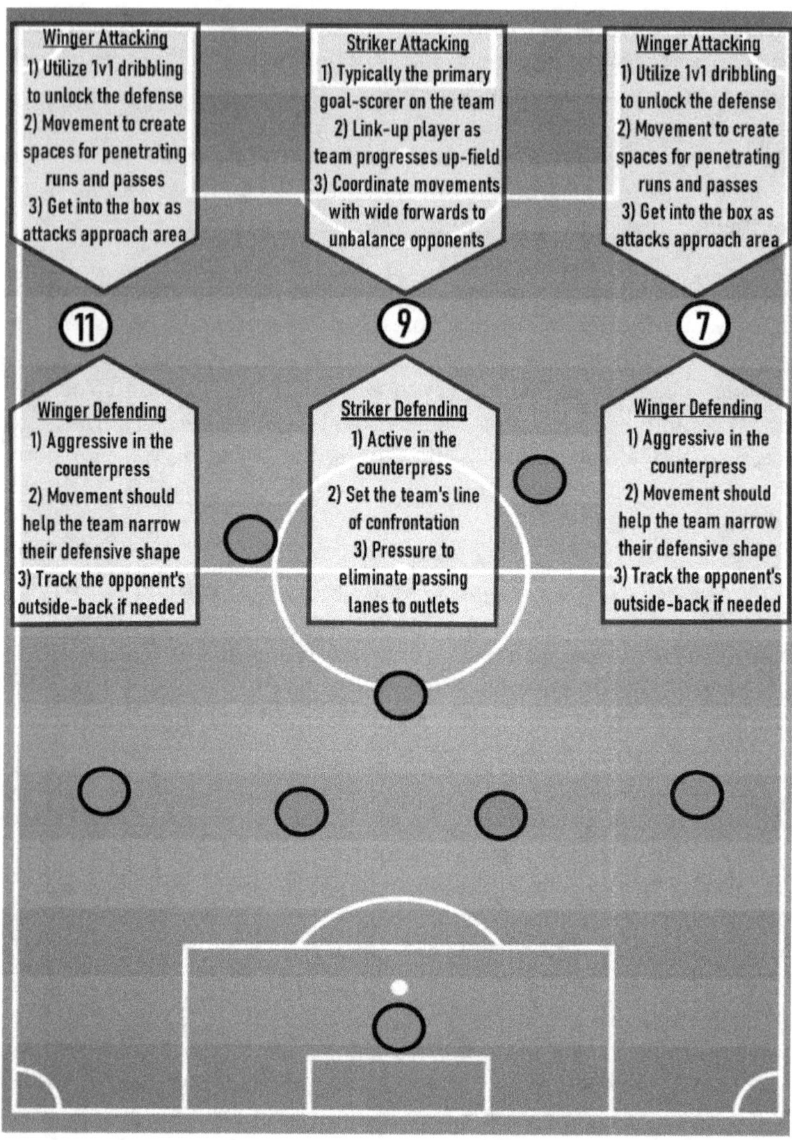

Center Forward - Center forwards can play a wide variety of roles within the team's tactics. For example, if Caroline is a taller, stronger player who can fend off opponents, she might serve as a target player. As the name suggests, she's a clear, high target that her teammates can play into. With her size and strength, a true 50/50 ball becomes a 75/25 chance of success. Deep-lying forwards are a close relative, but they'll look to receive in a lower part of the field, often on the ground while showcasing attacking midfielder type qualities.

There are also false #9s, who operate more like #10s, interacting with the midfield. By dropping into the midfield, the false #9 can pull an opposing centerback into the midfield, creating better passing lanes for the wide forwards to run into.

In a two forward formation, one might be more of a target player while the other is more of a second striker, which has many of the same creative responsibilities as a deep-lying forward.

The last two types we'll mention are the attacking forward and poachers. An attacking forward leads the line, often looking to run behind the defenders to stretch and disconnect them on the vertical axis. A poacher, as the name implies, hunts for goals and little else. The similarity between the two is that players with these roles tend to score a very high percentage of their team's goals. In a sense, they're the focal point when an attacking action is directed towards goal.

Finally, from a defensive standpoint, the game has moved in a direction where everyone must contribute defensively. Only players with otherworldly talent escape those demands, and that's an objectively small percentage. Unless your child is a Cristiano Ronaldo or Messi-type talent, defensive work is required. In fact, a center forward with excellent defensive output can often create her own chances on goal. Yes, scoring is the primary aim, but tactical and skill development tunnel vision is a dangerous approach. The modern game requires contribution in all phases of the game, so players should train and study that way.

Summary

1. Goalkeepers and defenders operate as the last lines of defense. They see the whole pitch and should use their voices to direct their teammates.
2. Midfielders are the link between the defensive and forward lines, controlling the flow and tempo of the game.
3. Forwards will score the bulk of the goals, but the modern

game requires them to engage defensively as well.

Style of Play

Style of play is a major talking point at the youth club level. Go to any club's website or talk to a director or coach about their style of play and we can just about guarantee you'll see or hear something to the effect of "we/I like to play an attacking style with lots of possession." You've probably heard it so often you are now numb to the words. Quite frankly, so have a fair share of clubs and coaches.

So what does "style of play" really mean?

In this section, our objective is to present some of the more common playing styles and clarify exactly what they mean. That way, the next time a club tells you they teach an attacking, possession-based style of play but then you catch their teams smashing long balls to the big, fast athlete up top, you'll know that something is rotten in the state of Denmark.

Note that in many cases, a team's playing style is a direct result of their coach's approach, which may or may not align with the club's playing philosophy. In these cases, it is the coach that's responsible for the style of play of that specific team, but the club has to identify the departure from their philosophy and help the coach realign his approach.

Direct

Route 1

Let's start with the most common form of direct soccer, the infamous Route 1 philosophy. This is a clear "win now" approach that pushes player development to the wayside. To put it in simple terms, the fastest route is from point A to point B. A Route 1 team will attack on that straight line, looking to use the speed and athleticism of the forwards to get past the opponent and through to goal.

This requires absolutely no soccer intelligence, just an athletic advantage up top and a couple of mistakes from the defending team. It's the perfect win-now approach because it focuses on keeping defenders behind the ball and risking very little in the attack.

The reason we're so critical of this style of play at the youth level is that it sacrifices player development for the sake of a few wins in early childhood. Yes, this may work at the younger and lower levels of play, but it's not a sustainable playing philosophy or player development model. Quality teams learn how to play against this style. Athletic advantages are also easier to nullify as growth spurts kick in, leveling the playing field.

With such low tactical and soccer IQ demands, even the top players in these systems are typically average to below-average players by U15s or U16s. If your child wants to even entertain the possibility of playing the game at a higher level, be it at a regional or national club level or collegiately, a more intelligent and technically demanding program is a necessity.

Direct Possession

Far from the "kick and run" of Route 1 soccer, direct possession maintains the lethal vertical qualities while also requiring players to engage in a more technically and tactically demanding approach. Rather than playing over the defenders and hoping your forward can outrun them, direct possession is typically a fast-paced attacking style that aggressively passes through the opposition's lines and engages in 1v1 duels in a very intentional manner.

Players with exceptional dribbling abilities are especially fond of this approach. Since the ball finds them quicker than an indirect possession style, your team's best dribblers often find themselves in 1v1 situations with running room in the wings. With additional space and isolation against the defender, the attacker can use his strength in the dribble against the outside-back or a covering centerback.

In the big picture, when the team attacks the opposition, they do so in a controlled and fast-paced manner. Another way to put it is teams are taking the space while it's still there. Direct possession is a high-tempo approach that acts on immediately available advantages.

Indirect

Indirect Possession

Moving from direct to indirect possession, which some call tiki taka, the major differences between the two are the tempo of the game, use of width, and the incorporation of deeper players, like outside-backs. Building out of the back and connecting the lines is central to the team's play. They'll look to unbalance the opposition's defense through possession, gradually creating the spaces they want to attack.

By overloading near the ball, which you'll recall means they're committing more numbers near the ball, the plan is to draw opponents away from desired attacking spaces. Once opponents are unbalanced, leaving large gaps in their defensive structure, that cues the next stage of the attack, often a line-breaking pass. Regardless of the attacking phase, these teams move up and down the pitch together.

Indirect build-out to direct attack

A hybrid of indirect and direct possession, the indirect build-out to direct attack is seen amongst teams that heavily emphasize building out of the back. Building out of the back is their means of widening the gaps in the opponent's defensive structure.

As the attacking team passes the ball near their own goal, they're trying to coax the defending team to commit more numbers higher up the field. Once the defending team is vertically unbalanced, leaving large gaps between the lines in their formation, the attacking team quickly plays the ball forward, initiating a lightning-quick attack to goal.

It's a high-risk, high-reward style. The goalkeeper, defenders, and midfielders must be especially proficient with the ball, or this style of play backfires.

Positional Play

While positional play is very closely linked to indirect possession, there's more of an emphasis on what's happening off the ball, particularly in the way a team manages space. A central theme in positional play is the strategic starting points of the players within the system with X number of players in each vertical channel, X in the horizontal lines as determined by the coach. Maximizing the space a team occupies is the key. You'll find overloads near the ball, but the positioning of the players outside of that cluster is what allows for ball progression.

Transition

Counterattacking

One of the common mistakes you'll find on the sidelines, both of them really, is equating counterattacking with Route 1, or vice versa. The difference between the two is in the sense of purpose in progression (rather than playing the odds that you'll get on the end of one of ten long balls) and the precision of the attack. Let's face it, even if your kid's team is excellent in possession, there will come a game when the opponent is the stronger possessing squad or something's just not clicking, and that's okay. It happens.

When possession is unfruitful, it's up to the team to find another solution. That's typically where counterattacking comes into play. As the opponent's attacking shape expands, covering the majority of the attacking half of the field, gaps emerge. Huge gaps! That's when the counterattack is on. Counterattacks are precise moves up the field with little to no excess. Keep time and passes to a minimum, just work together to advance to goal ASAP.

Defensive Approaches

Soccer is a battle of initiatives. If there's a clear stronger team, they'll look to set the game's initiative through their attacking play, whereas the weaker team will do so through defensive tactics, which cover a wide range. We'll give you one example of transitional defending and three from open play.

Counterpressing

Jürgen Klopp, currently the Liverpool coach in the English Premier League (EPL), is famous for his counterpressing, even going so far as to say goal-scoring opportunities from the counterpress are of higher quality than those from a playmaker. In essence, counterpressing is pressing the opposition's counterattack.

When a team counterattacks, their objective is to progress up the field as quickly as possible. Counterpressing targets the opponent's forward momentum. For example, let's say the blue team has the ball, then loses it to the red team. The red players rush forward in an attempt to counterattack, but blue pressures the ball carrier and wins it back. Half of the red team outran the ball and are now out of position to defend, whereas the blue team committed numbers towards the ball. Blue now has more numbers running towards the red goal than the red team. Counterpressing, pressing the counterattack, helped blue turn a threat into a massive advantage.

High Press/Middle block/Low block

When coaches and analysts talk about presses or blocks, they're talking about where the defense is positioned and engaging the opponent.

A high press is when the defending team engages the opponent in the highest third (attacking third) of the field. In other words, the defending team likely has everyone in the attacking team's half of the field. The objective is to win the ball as close to the opponent's goal as possible.

A middle block means the defending team is set up in the middle third of the pitch. They're encouraging the opponent to get into their expansive, attacking shape while also reducing the space between the defenders and goalie. Less space between them means the opponent has less space to run into.

A low block is when a team defends in their defensive third, roughly the 30-40 yards closest to their own goal. They don't want to leave any space between their defenders and goalie, typically because of a wide gap in quality between the two teams. It's also a common end-of-game tactic for winning teams.

In fewer words, high/middle/low refer to the thirds of the field. High press → attacking third, middle block → middle third, and low block → defensive third.

So which is best?

A team's primary style of play will likely come from a club-wide philosophy or their coach. On a secondary level, the team must adapt to the players on the field and the qualities of the opponent. A single game could see a team use several of these tactics, but that doesn't mean they've abandoned their philosophy. The primary style of play is at the core, whereas the secondary is a response to the context of the game. It's problem-solving, adaptability, and an exercise in soccer IQ.

Summary

1. Direct play is fine so long as there is a clear sense of purpose and a reasonably high chance of success in the individual actions, which only rules out Route 1 play, which is an inhibitor to player development.
2. Indirect play is probably the most aesthetically pleasing, but possession dominance does require teams to attack against more organized defenses, increasing the level of difficultly to goal.
3. Teams can look to initiate play through defense, but this is typically only asked of professional, amateur, and high or older-level youth teams. Most youth teams should be relentless in attack regardless of the scoreline.

Formations

What's the purpose of formations?

Now that we've discussed styles of play, it's time to move onto formations. If the style of play gave a meta impression, you might find yourself thinking that the style of play precedes the formation. If so, you're exactly right.

Coaches, players, and analysts spend a lot of time talking about formations, so it might surprise you that some other aspect is more important to a team's play. You might even ask, "if style of play comes before formations, then what are formations for?"

Glad you asked.

Formations assist in executing the team's philosophy, their style of play. The basic function of a formation is to create time and space to execute the team's style of play while denying/limiting the opponent. In that sense, formations are little more than numbers on a page.

Formations Are How You Manage the Game

Look closely enough and you'll see most teams use different formations when attacking vs defending. The formations that we speak of, like a 1-4-4-2 or a 1-4-3-3, often represent a team's defensive setup. Attacking formations can take an entirely different shape. Real Madrid often use a 1-2-2-6, whereas Manchester City opt for more coverage with a 1-2-3-5. Over in the Portuguese league, Porto might run a 1-4-4-2 on paper, but the attacking shape looks more like a 1-2-5-3.

Each team has different objectives. RB Leipzig coach Julian Nagelsmann wants to overload and dominate the central part of the field, so his team uses a midfield square with two forwards and two centerbacks on either side of the mids. That gives him eight players in the center of the field, which allows him to counterpress effectively and overload near the ball in attack.

In layman's terms, start with the end in mind. Once you understand the "what" and the "why", numbers and personnel are placed in specific areas and roles to fit the overall philosophy.

The beauty of this approach is that in narrowing the scope of each player's responsibilities, the tactical limitations define their role and allow them to act quicker and more freely once they see their fit within the big picture. Like painting, the coach is adding a layer at a time, defining phases of play and positional responsibilities within each layer of the team's tactics.

Don't take this chapter as saying formations aren't important. They do provide structure and offer a mental image for the players and coaches.

Each formation is easily tailored to the team's style of play, but there are some general approaches linked to each formation. With that in mind, let's look at five of the most common formations in the modern game.

Most Common Formations

1-4-3-3

A very attack-oriented formation, the 1-4-3-3 is designed for relentless attacking. This formation has three high targets to keep the opponent's backline honest, dedicates three players to the center of the midfield, and creates a gap in the wings that outside-backs can attack. The three midfielders will generally form a triangle in the center of the field, often with two attacking center-mids.

Defensively, this formation allows teams to commit more numbers to the high press and counterpress. If the high press is broken, there are some defensive vulnerabilities in the formation.

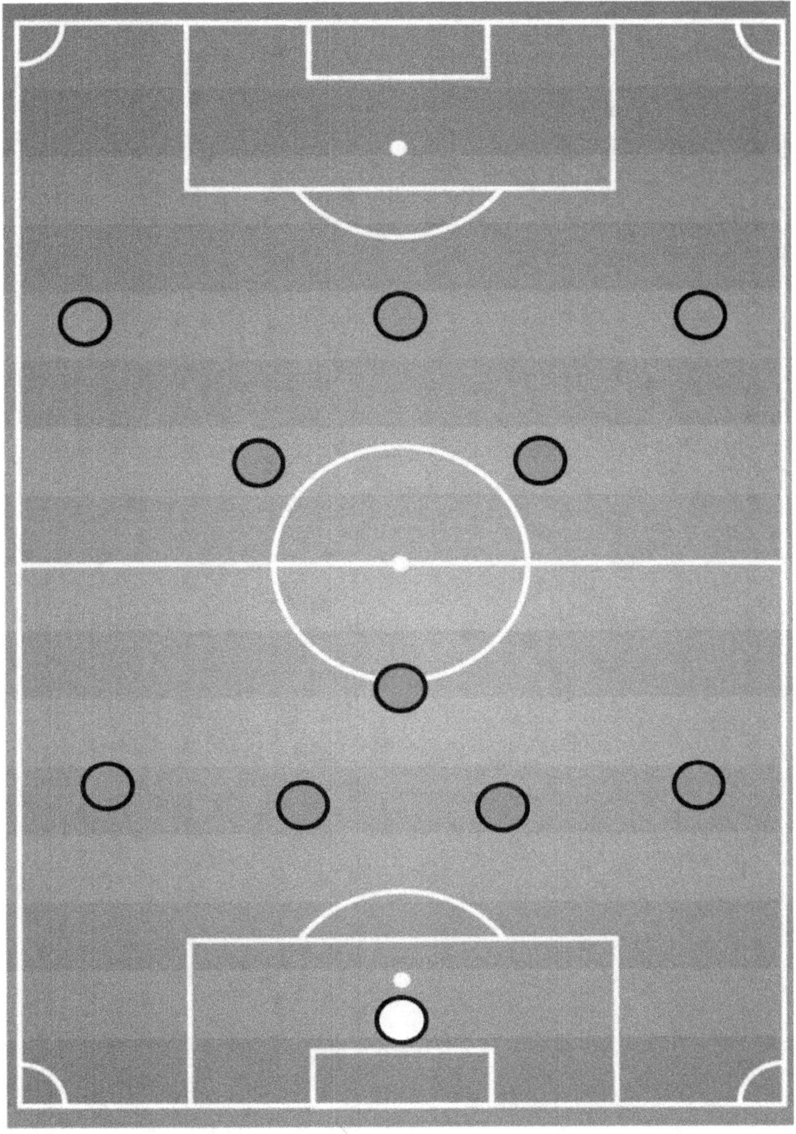

1-4-2-3-1

A variant of the 1-4-3-3, the 1-4-2-3-1 uses many of the same attacking dynamics in the wings. It's the central channel and half spaces where we see the greatest difference. With two defensive central midfielders, defensive solidity is prioritized over midfield attacking contributions. That said, if your team has a brilliant playmaker in midfield, they can really excel within that lone center attacking mid role (#10).

The biggest advantage of the formation is having two central defensive midfielders to protect the two centerbacks. Since the central spaces offer the most direct and quickest path to goal, protecting this space is a top priority. Two defensive center mids protect that part of the field, which, in turn, gives more attacking freedom to the forward, attacking midfielders, and outside-backs.

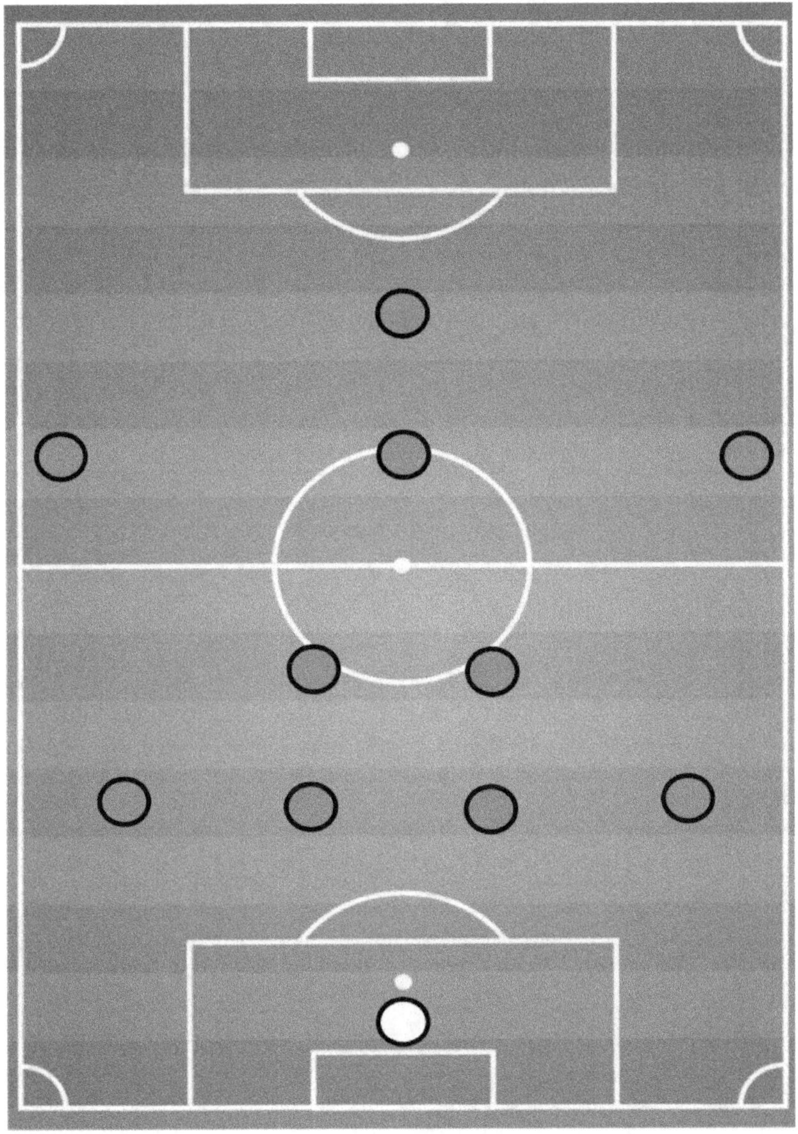

1-4-4-2

Typically associated with a more defensive style of play, the 1-4-4-2 is generally used either for the two banks of four players along the midfield and defensive lines or because that's the formation we all grew up playing. Seriously, it's the only one our club teams used. Those two lines of four, especially when defending in a low block, are really difficult to play around.

When the midfield is flat, spanning the width of the field, it connects the outside-backs and wide midfielders. If a diamond midfield is chosen, teams can overload the middle to clear the wings for the outside-backs.

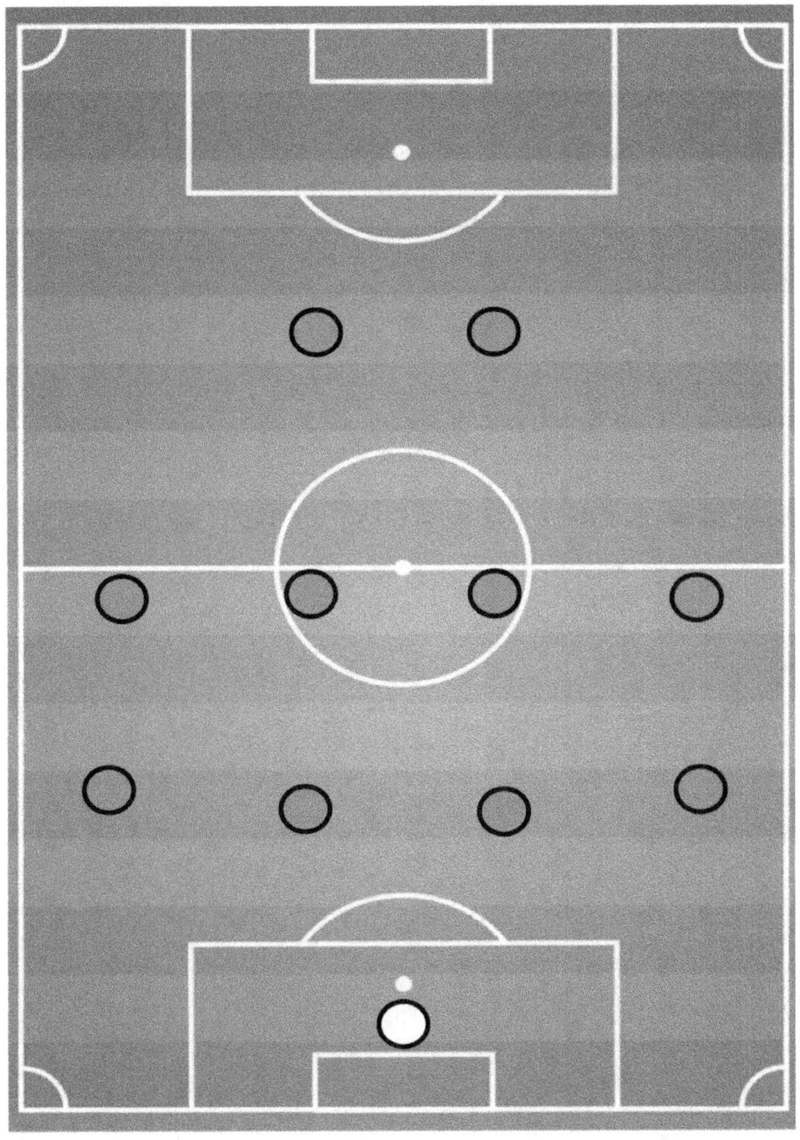

1-3-5-2

A staple in the Italian soccer world, 1-3-5-2 is a nice option for teams that want to dominate the central area of the pitch. Three centerbacks offer excellent protection at one end of the formation while to center forwards can play off of each other up top. If the two forwards are up against the back four, that will also leave them 2v2 in the middle of the field, a major threat for the opposition.

In midfield, you'll often see three center mids sometimes layered, sometimes flat, with two wide midfielders. one of the beauties of this formation is that it easily converts to a 1-5-3-2 if the team is under duress. The two wide midfielders can also join the backline to make it a back five while the three midfielders become very compact in front of them. You can also have one of the two forwards drop into the midfield to make it a 1-5-4-1.

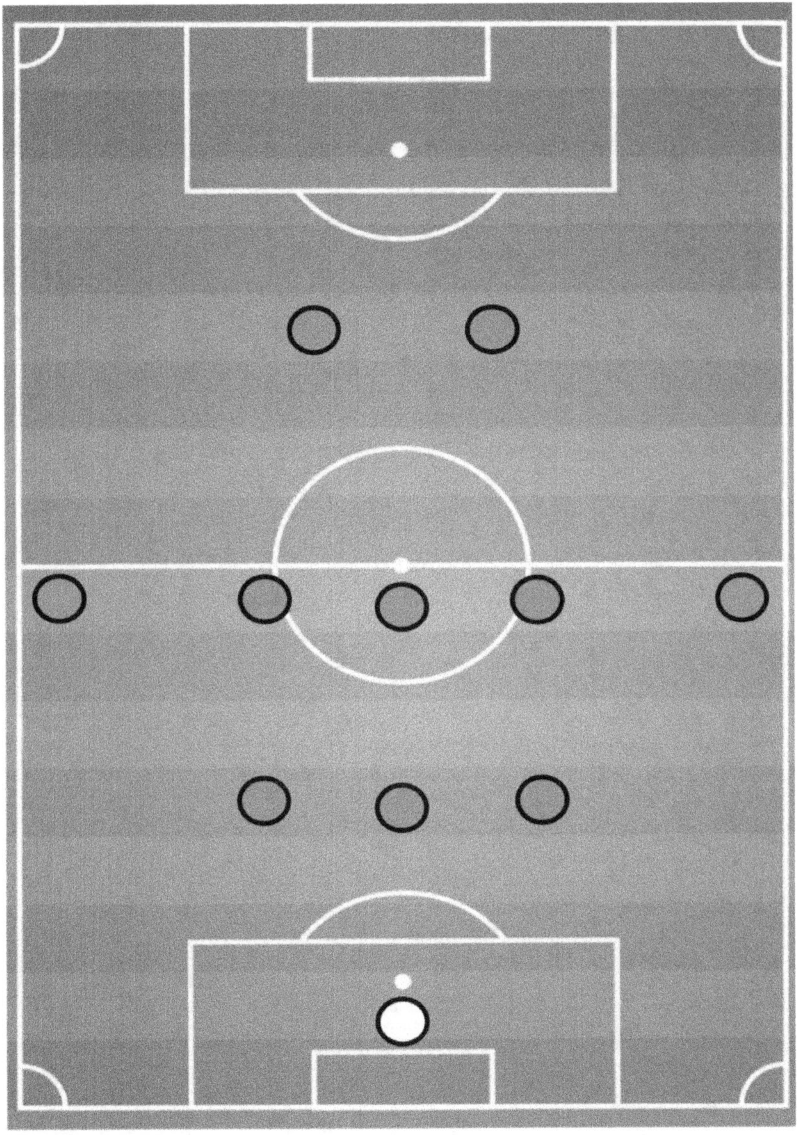

1-3-4-3

A very attack-oriented formation, the 1-3-4-3 is well-suited for teams with two ball-winning central midfielders, three dominant centerbacks, and a combination of clever forwards who can work off of each other to create gaps in the opposition's defense. With numbers high up the pitch, this is a great formation for counterpressing and high pressing.

The greatest variation in this formation is in how a coach uses the three forwards, especially in relation to the two wide midfielders. If the forwards play more narrowly, possibly with the central forward dropping into a false #9 role to take up a spot in the midfield, then the wings are wide open for the two wide attacking mids. If a coach sets the midfield more narrowly or even in a diamond, you'd likely see two of the forwards take up width provider roles, but this is far less common.

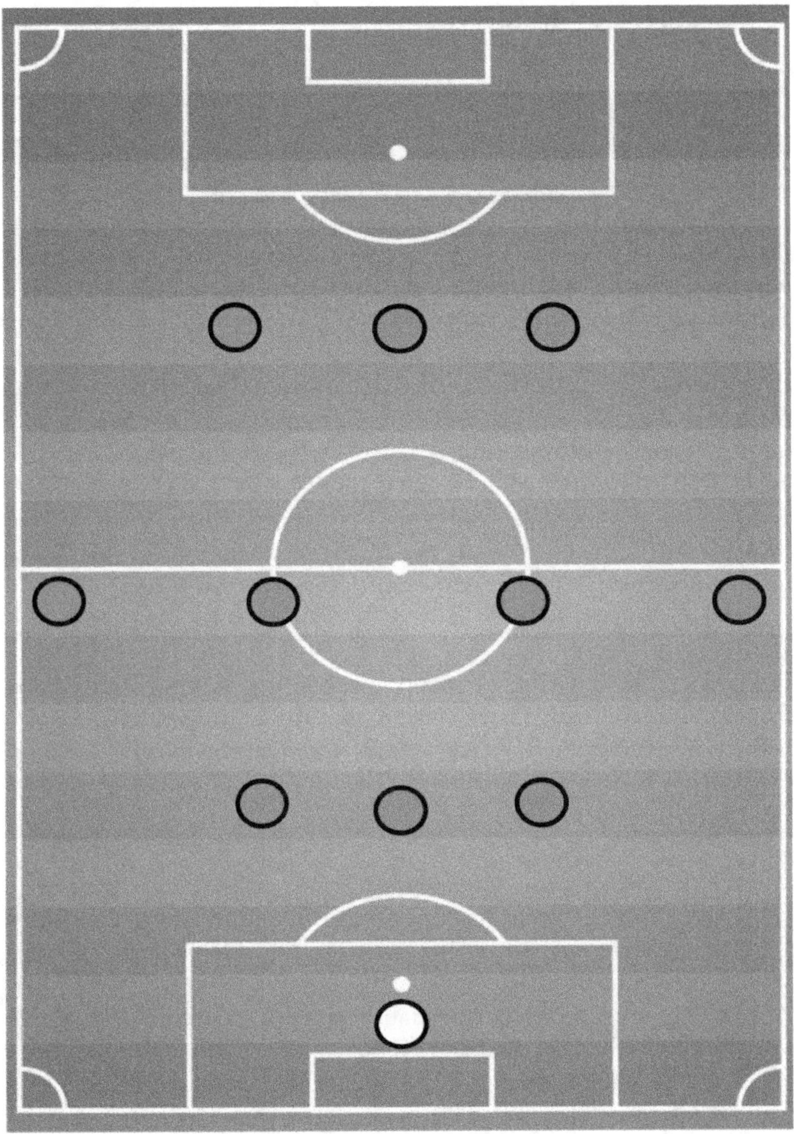

Formations Serve the Style of Play

When trying to figure out a team's formation, it's easiest to pick out in the defensive phases of the game or, especially at the youth level, during a kickoff. If you aren't able to catch the kickoff, just watch the way teams set up defensively. Are there four defenders or three? How many forwards do they have? If two, you'll likely find them in the middle of the field. If it looks like they have high and wide players on either side of the field, they're likely playing with three forwards or some variation of a 1-4-3-3.

Regardless of the way the team is set out, the biggest point is that formations are the way coaches fit their personnel to the team's style of play. Scott's had unbalanced teams with just one natural outside-back, so he transitioned to a back three because he had depth at centerback. Some coaches will tell you they don't have a true center forward, a #9. In those cases, you might see them use a 1-4-3-3, but use a more creative player as the center forward while using her as a creative midfielder (#10).

Just remember that the formation is not the system. Rather, the formation serves the system. Style of play is the foundation, the formation is simply how the coach and players initially position themselves to carry out the philosophy.

Summary

1. Formations are how you manage the game, fitting the team's shape to allow for the greatest possible success of your player personnel.
2. There's no objectively right or wrong formation. It simply has to fit the available players.
3. It's easiest to pick out the opposing team's formation during kickoffs and when they're defending. Figuring out the number of defenders and forwards they're playing with will help you find your answer.

Tactics

All right, so we've had our chapter on style of play/philosophy, then a conversation about formations. Now there's a chapter on tactics? What's the difference? Do we even need to make a distinction?

Yes, we absolutely do.

From our experience, this is one of the greatest misconceptions among coaches, players, and parents. A style of play or philosophy is the endpoint. In determining our overarching approach to the game, we're essentially identifying the way we think a game should be played. In other words, the style of play has the end in mind.

Formations, as just discussed, are how a coach fits his personnel on the field to carry out the style of play. Any number of formations can carry out any number of playing philosophies. The big point is that formations consider personnel and put them in the best position to carry out the philosophy.

So, now we have tactics. If the style of play is the big picture, tactics are the specific actions we take to reach the endpoint. As Sun Tzu wrote in *The Art of War*, "strategy without tactics is the slowest route to victory. Tactics without strategy is the noise before defeat." The underlying philosophy determines the basic approach, but it's through tactics that we find small advantages within the style of play, especially if we have the opportunity to measure our team's tactics against the opponents.

If we know how they play or which tactical devices they're likely to use, it's easier to tailor our approach to gain the upper hand. After all, soccer is an invasion sport, a term with martial origins. It's not simply a battle of systems and formations. It's also a matter of identifying the strengths and weaknesses of each team and adapting to the matchup. Throughout the game, the players and coach must determine how to amplify their strengths and attack the opponent's weaknesses, all the while minimizing their own vulnerabilities, especially those that are directly attacked by the opponent's strengths.

Four Reference Points (Ball, Teammates, Opponents, Space)

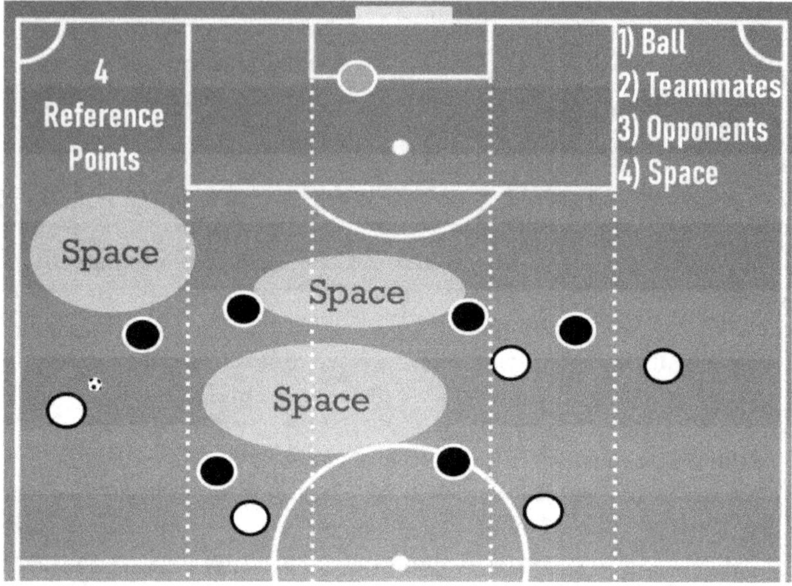

When it comes to the tactical side of the game, whether they know it or not, the players and coaches are making their adjustments to four reference points.

The first is the ball.

The location of the ball will not only have a team-wide implication for positioning, but it should also send certain cues to each individual player as well. If I'm the left-back and the opponents have the ball on the right-wing, I need to slide into the middle of the field so I can stay connected to my centerbacks. If I'm the goalkeeper, I want to draw a straight line from the middle of the goal to the ball and stay on that straight line so that my positioning gives me the best shot-stopping angle.

Second, you have teammates.

This is where it's so important for coaches to speak with their players individually. If a coach can create a position-specific roadmap for the player, then recreate that image through exercises and games, then a player can see where they fit in relation to their teammates. Having a strong sense of positional understanding and how they fit into the big picture, each player uses that defined role as the default for action. Within that default, the path forward becomes more apparent. As positional clarity is achieved, you see the player use their understanding of their positional sense to more freely express themselves within the team's tactics. Understanding is the root of intelligent action.

Third, we have the opponents.

Some of the smartest players we've seen in this regard were defensive central midfielders. During his first coaching years, there was one girl on Scott's team, we'll call her Mia, who was exceptional in this regard. Turns out she was also a basketball player during the winter months. Scott could clearly see the influence of a tighter, more compact game like basketball on her approach to scanning for opponents and finding pockets of space in soccer. It really is a matter of identifying imbalances within the opponent's structure (Are they bunching near the ball? Where are the gaps?) and responding to claim an advantage.

Another great example of this is a forward who pulls his defender away from help to create a passing lane into the space he wants to attack. Move the defender and you create your own opportunities.

Finally, our *fourth* reference point is space.

While the other three point to tangible objects, this fourth reference point is trying to find the absence of people. Obviously, it's very closely tied to the other reference points, especially teammates and the opponent, but this is where you really see how mentally engaged the player is. Are they frequently scanning the field, looking for little pockets of space that buy them additional time? Do they know what they're looking for? When they see a better pocket of space, are they quick to fill it and connect their body orientation to the current position of the ball and the action they want to undertake once they've received the pass?

The players who are strongest in managing these reference points, continuously evaluating the field and reconstructing their mental image of the reference points, are often the most influential in a team. That's not to say we wouldn't take the youth soccer version of Usain Bolt on our youth teams, allowing him to use his freakish athleticism to run behind defenders, but those players with high soccer IQs are the ones who make the play happen. They're the ones who connect the lines and deliver that final pass. Often overlooked, these players are the heartbeat of the team.

Superiorities (Numerical, Positional, Qualitative, Socio-affective)

The final area we'll address in this chapter is superiorities. Let's start with a clarification. By superiorities, we're not talking about an egotistical, inflated view of oneself. Rather, we're looking at it from the perspective that if we can identify an exploit situations that favor our team or our player, we can then use the circumstances to break the game open. Simply put, superiorities are conditions that favor our team instead of the opposition.

As with the reference points, there are four superiorities.

The first of which is numerical superiority.

When we speak of overloads, this is the point we're trying to drive home. Attacking teams look to create a numerical superiority in order to better their chances of breaking the opposition's defensive structure. This is especially important for possession-based teams. Since the game moves a little bit slower for them if the opponent is well-organized, they often look for numerical superiorities to beat the first line of the press.

From a defensive standpoint, more numbers near or behind the ball typically increases your odds of a recovery. At the very least, you are in a favorable position to deny a goal-scoring opportunity.

Second, there's a positional superiority.

This one's more difficult to pick out than numerical superiority. In order to identify a positional superiority, you have to have an understanding of which team is better positioned within the current context of the game. Say your team is dominating possession, but the opponent has everyone behind the ball. In that situation, you'd probably say the opponent has a positional superiority because they're well suited to deny space and limit your chances on goal.

Now, flip the sides and say your team is more counterattack-based. If the other team is in an expansive attacking shape and has basically given you the entire middle of the field to counterattack, the positional superiority is on your side.

The best question to ask is, which team is more organized and better suited to accomplish their attacking or defensive objectives? Whichever team that is, they hold the positional superiority.

Third, there's the qualitative superiority.

You know that team that has that one really special player? You give that player the ball and they're guaranteed to beat one, two, maybe even three players on their own. That's an example of a qualitative superiority. That player's supreme individual talent is so far beyond the playing field that at times you almost just feel they need to get the ball at their feet and unleash the magic.

Now, a qualitative superiority goes beyond simple 1v1s. For example, if I have three players near the ball in the middle of the field against three of the opposition's players, but mine make the better trio, I have a qualitative advantage.

To take an example from the NFL, if I had prime Joe Montana and prime Jerry Rice on my team, I really wouldn't care who you have on your defensive line and at cornerback. I'm going to beat you. Simple as that. Whatever quality you can muster, my two guys are far more impressive and influential.

Our fourth superiority is the socio-affective.

You know those players who when they're on the fields or the court together just seem to have an amazing understanding of each other.

Together, they earn an A+ in chemistry, at least in soccer. They might not have as much talent as the two opponents they're up against, but the understanding they have of each other gives them such a remarkable advantage.

That's an example of a socio-affective superiority. One of the things we like to do is find players who either have a similar understanding of the game or are great friends off the field and put them on the same part of the pitch together. The chemistry they have is such a massive advantage.

As coaches adjust their tactics to meet the demands of specific games and matchups, they're trying to help players interpret the four reference points and respond in a way that creates superiorities. Tactics fit hand in hand with the style of play and are expressed through the formation. In-game adaptation is a recognition of opportunities and vulnerabilities. That's where the tactical adjustments come in.

Summary
1. Style of play/philosophy determines the big picture approach, whereas tactics are the small details that adapt to the game as a team searches for advantages.
2. There are four reference points: 1) the ball, 2) teammates, 3) opponents, and 4) space.
3. There are also four types of superiorities: 1) numerical, 2) positional, 3) qualitative, and 4) socio-affective.

Key Coaches & Their Influence

Soccer was first professionalized in the 1880s. In its long history, the rules, styles of play, and tactics have undergone significant changes.

For instance, the 1-2-3-5 is one of the earliest soccer formations. Those two defenders were called full-backs (because they were fully back) and the three in the middle were called half backs (because they were half back players, half forward players). Clever, weren't they?

We see those origins in the modern game. In England and parts of the USA, people still refer to outside-backs as full-backs. That's because the 1-3-2-5 was the next progression. The full-backs were split into wide parts of the field and the center-half (what we call a centerback) dropped in between the two full-backs. Though the names full-back and center-half are misnomers of a bygone era, they do point us in the direction of tactical development in the history of the game.

The modern game is largely a progression of Brazil's O Jogo Bonito (The Beautiful Game) and Dutch Total Football. In this chapter, we'll highlight some of the top influencers in the modern game, starting with the Dutch school of thought.

Johan Cruyff - Student of Rinus Michels

Total Football. You've probably heard the term before. In fact, your two authors met through Total Football Analysis, a soccer tactics website and magazine dedicated to the finer ideas of the game.

Originating from a meeting of the minds in 1965 Amsterdam, Johan Cruyff, the field general and star of Ajax, welcomed Rinus Michels, a general of a coach. These fathers of the modern game devised a style of play predicated on high-tempo attacking play and intense defensive transitions. While they certainly had their own tactical influences, it's these two who revolutionized the game, bringing it into the modern era.

The Total Football system required interaction and rotations unseen in the history of the game. Pele's Brazilian teams had started using attacking outside-backs, but it's the Ajax and Barcelona teams of Cruyff and Michels that took the idea to the next level.

Cruyff himself was a forward, but often dropped deep to receive the ball and dictate play. His actions spurred a response from his teammates, creating confusion for the opposition. Soccer IQ, tactical depth, and technical competence of all players are hallmarks of the system.

Pep Guardiola - Student of Johan Cruyff

You know those Barcelona "tiki taka" teams from the early part of the 2000s? Their origin is in Cruyff's Total Football.

Both Michels and Cruyff moved to Barcelona after their time at Ajax. Cruyff in particular revolutionized the famed La Masia academy at Barcelona...twice! The greatest compliment we can give these two coaches is to say that the modern game is a footnote to their pioneering thoughts.

While at Barcelona, Cruyff coached a young defensive midfielder (tactical #6) by the name of Pep Guardiola. In terms of soccer philosophies, Cruyff couldn't have looked into a philosophical mirror and seen a closer reflection. Guardiola was to Cruyff what Cruyff was the Michels.

Though "tiki taka" is the term most often ascribed to Guardiola, positional play is more accurate. As Adin Osmanbašić, founder of the tactics website Spielverlagerung, says in his authoritative article, "Positional Play is a philosophy that has many principles but the fundamental principle is the search for superiority." Highly structured with very defined positional responsibilities, the narrowed scope helps teams create and then attack the right situations.

Extreme possession percentages compliment the style. The idea is that if my team has the ball, the other team can't score. In this regard, possession is as much a defensive tool as it is an attacking one.

Frustrated opponents, tired of chasing the ball, will then likely lose their defensive compactness and concede high-quality scoring opportunities.

José Mourinho - Student of Vitor Frade

Often labeled as "anti-football" (or anti-soccer), José Mourinho is known for his deep, compact defending and lightning-quick counterattacks. Referring back to previous coaching influences, Helenio Herrera is one. The legendary Italian coach is famed for his hard-nosed defensive approach at Inter Milan.

From a tactical perspective, that model fits Mourinho's. Often quoted for his references to the cost of mistakes in soccer, Mourinho's style of play is based on restricting the number of mistakes his team makes while baiting the opposition into overcommitting in attack. To accomplish that feat, Mourinho's teams have famously positioned themselves deep in their half of the field, even committing all 11 players within 30 yards of their own goal, which is what the term "parking the bus" refers to. Leave no space for opponents to attack, limit risks when in possession, and then strike quickly on the counterattack to score goals.

In a more holistic sense, Mourinho's greatest influence is a sports science professor from Porto University by the name of Vítor Frade. Tactical periodization is Frade's greatest contribution to the game, which has spread through the large number of influential Portuguese coaches in the game. Through macro and micro cycles, clubs rotate training topics irrespective of match outcomes. The purpose is developing well-rounded players rather than taking a short-sighted approach and simply fixing the latest issues.

It's the highly defensive, quick counterattacking, and systemic approach to training that propelled Mourinho to the top of the profession. Just to clarify, wherever he's coached, the first team has taken this win-now approach while the youth teams have prioritized individual player development over early, youth wins. Mourinho himself has been critical of nations that don't holistically develop youth players, either through pigeonholing players in one position or neglecting player development to win ugly in youth matches.

To be clear, Mourinho, like most great managers, believes youth players must prioritize the ideas taught at practices, then show a relentlessly competitive mentality to outperform the opponent, which is where winning factors into the youth game. Show commitment to the process and fight like a warrior, a very Northern Portuguese mentality to life and soccer.

Jürgen Klopp - Student of Wolfgang Frank

When Guardiola joined Bayern Munich back in 2013, he was taken aback by the pressing and quick counterattacking of the German Bundesliga. His main rival was a coach by the name of Jürgen Klopp.

The German comes from a long line of tactical innovators. Michels and Cruyff inspired Arrigo Sacchi's zonal pressing systems, which led to Wolfgang Frank's adaptation of pressing within a back four without a sweeper (commonplace now, but wildly unpopular as recently as the 1990s). That, in turn, led to Ralf Rangnick's counterpressing, a theory which Klopp has perfected.

Counterpressing is the act of pressing the ball in the transition from attacking to defending. In essence, it's countering the opposition's counterattack. We hope your youth coach knows this is the most influential aspect of the game he can coach to prevent goals and create your team's own scoring chances. Klopp himself calls counterpressing his best playmaker. To backup the point, Klopp's Liverpool averaged 7.81 seconds of possession and an average of 2.51 passes en route to a UEFA Champions League title in 2019.

Why's that?

Think about it. Let's say my team has just stolen the ball from yours about 30 yards from our goal. We're pretty far from your goal, but there's lots of space in front of us. We decide to attack that space quickly through a counterattack. The issue is that we don't have many high targets, so our forwards and attacking midfielders have to sprint up the field before they're realistic passing options.

But while my team was flying up the field, your team counterpressed and won the ball. All of a sudden, my team's out of position and our momentum is moving in the wrong direction. Meanwhile, your team is heading straight to goal with fewer defenders to beat. Plus, since you've quickly reduced your coverage area, your players are now tightly connected, creating numerical superiorities against my scattered team. That's the impact Klopp has brought to the game. His quick counterpressing and lightning-quick attacks on goal are so dangerous.

Zinedine Zidane - Student of Marcelo Lippi

Finally, we have Zinedine Zidane. Widely regarded as a top 10 player of all-time, even top 5 in some circles, Zidane is the King of Cool on the touchline. Scott's book, Revitalizing Real Madrid, gives an in-depth look at Zidane's 2019/20 tactics, but the two underlying qualities Zidane brings to the game are almost soft skills. Tactical adaptation and man-management (the way he interacts with the players) are the two qualities that help him get the most out of his team.

Much like his Italian influencers, Marcelo Lippi and Carlo Ancelotti, defensive structure is the focal point, which then frees the creatives higher up the pitch to play to their strengths. His two recent contributions to soccer tactics are the central square in rest defense (centerbacks and defensive midfielders forming a square when Real Madrid has possession of the ball) and a man-marking high press.

As an all-time great, Zidane knows that the most important battle is in the mind. Especially with elite players, the right mental framework allows them to impose their quality on lesser opponents.

Summary
1. Johan Cruyff and Rinus Michels are the fathers of modern soccer, transforming the game with Total Football.
2. Pep Guardiola's positional play revived a high-paced, possession-based approach.
3. José Mourinho, a long-time, direct rival to Pep, brought a more pragmatic, defensive approach to counter Guardiola's philosophy. These coaches have defined 21st-century soccer.

SECTION THREE:
The Playing Experience

Choosing & Switching Clubs

According to Zillow, families invest 11 hours researching a car purchase and 8 hours researching a vacation. Most families don't spend much time researching clubs though they often spend $5-20K, the cost of a used car, at the classic level over 3-5 years. The kids will likely spend more years at a club than a school.

Soccer clubs are filled with some of the hardest working and most caring people you will ever meet. Most are former soccer players who want to stay involved in the game and earn a living. Most clubs are non-profits who just barely make it. They are soccer people and generally not business people who get the nuances of customer-centric approaches. Executive Directors have a challenging time managing families, coaches, partners, and a board. They are often busy raising money for new facilities or organizing events.

Coaches are often juggling 2-3 teams, which come out to 25-55 players and families. Working lots of hours, they are expected to win from the club, coaches, players, and parents. Unfortunately, the desire to win may be more important to some than the development of the player. Coaches and clubs are in a quandary.

Choosing a club wisely requires some forethought and research. You can always course correct but it's a good idea to put in the effort first.

> **When you look at the statistics of retention, the alarming retention rates in America, 38.5% of kids who play soccer in America quit by the age of seven and another 50% quit by the age of 10. And then 70% of all kids in team sports in America quit by the age of 13. I have a pretty good feeling, it's not the good kids that are quitting. It's the kids that just don't develop well.**
>
> **-Tom Byer**

Considerations

Convenience

These factors, such as travel times, training times, location, and logistics, are usually the biggest considerations. Sibling schedules are also important.

Coaches

This is often the most valued consideration. If possible, chat to several parents about the coach's ability to develop player relationships and explain things simply. A prestigious playing career is second to those factors. Determining what level coaching badge they have also indicates what level of commitment the coach has to the profession. Note that two years is usually the most time you want your player with one coach.

Cost

This is self-explanatory.

Competitive Offering

Some families want clubs to have a pathway to college soccer. If this is the case, then ECNL level soccer is a must when the players are U15 and above.

Size

You may want a club that has several teams of differing ability in your player's age group. Some clubs are huge. Others are boutique. There is a spectrum of tradeoffs between the benefits of a large club (national prestige, better facilities, more competition) versus a small club (more individualized experience and lower cost).

Invest the time in researching by talking to many parents, especially those of older players. If possible, speak to the coaches or at least watch them and see how they manage a practice or game. Don't be dazzled by the good-looking uniforms or coaches' playing histories.

A good fit is key.

Changing Clubs

> **It's time to change clubs "when you feel that your child's development as a player is either stagnating or you feel like you are not getting the opportunities that you deserve. Most importantly, seek out the best coaching that you can get, because, in the end, your experience a lot of time is dependent on your coach.**
>
> **-Gary Buete**

Sometimes, the fit is not there. In our experiences, changing clubs is best after exhausting all the options at your current club. You have to advocate for your player while keeping in mind it's perfectly reasonable that coaches and clubs have to consider entire teams. Here is my escalation checklist.

1. If it is about a situation on the field, speak with the coach and ask what they think is needed to change. Avoid setting up a meeting before or after games. Try this approach no more than 2-3 times over as many months. Ideally, get a perspective from another coach about the situation.
2. Set up a meeting with an area director or executive director depending on the club's size.
3. Observe other club coaches during games and practices. Talk to parents of players of those clubs to get a feel for the coach.
4. Contact the admin of the other clubs to see what the steps are to move.
5. Make the decision realizing that the grass may seem greener on the other side.

Generally, don't make changes during the season. It is disruptive to the teams and can be a poor precedent for your player. Chris knows of a player whose family pulled them from several clubs over two seasons. In the end, no club would take the player. Avoid sharing the blow-by-blow of the changing experience with your player.

This process is hard and should be avoided if possible. However, you are the best advocate for your player assuming that you have realistic expectations of how capable your player is and what the club is capable of offering.

Summary

1. The average person spends 11 hours researching a new car purchase, but virtually no time researching youth soccer clubs, despite the fact that the youth soccer experience can cost as much as a new car.
2. Top considerations for choosing a club include convenience, coaches, cost, competitive offering, and the size of the club.
3. Poor fit can lead to the necessity of changing clubs. Don't do this during the season. Instead, use this time to explore your options through informational meetings and observing matches.

Reframing the Tryout Process

Here we are, everyone's least favorite time of the year, tryouts. Trust me, no one enjoys this. As parents of soccer players, we know how much anxiety it causes them and we share that burden.

On the flip side, the vast majority of coaches don't enjoy tryouts either. No one likes to tell a kid they're not moving up after a year of dedication and hard work. No one likes to send a kid down to a lower team because they were overwhelmed the previous season.

No one enjoys disappointing the kids, but even tryout disappointments start from a place of thoughtfulness. Maybe that promotion to the next team wasn't given, but not because the child's a bad player. We've seen a lot of kids who have really good qualities and were on the fringe of making the next team up, but that promotion simply didn't happen.

It's something to investigate on a case-by-case basis, but you'll often find one of three reasons as to why a player isn't promoted.

1. They need a little more time to develop other areas of their game

2. There's not a tactical or personnel need at that position

3. Some players are better suited staying down a level to improve their confidence and gain experience as a leading player before advancing a level

When you measure the difference between making Team A vs Team B, fringe players are often caught between the realities of joining the higher-rated team as a bench player and accepting a role on the lower team, but becoming one of the stars.

Each kid will respond differently. Some really enjoy the challenge of playing at a higher level, even if it means they're receiving very little playing time or just a fringe player in the team's tactics. Scott was caught in a scenario like this as a U10 playing up a year with the U11s. He saw that he was not essential to the team and his playing time was limited. So, while still playing at that age group the following season, which is because his club didn't have another U11 team in the fold, he did step back a level of play and became a key player on the team. Everything in the team's tactics went through him. It was the exact opposite of the previous season and exactly what he needed to restore his confidence and fall in love with the game again.

The reason we tell that story is because moving down a team or failing to gain promotion to the next level can actually come with many positives. We're big believers in the psychological aspects of the game, that confidence is one of the key qualities a player must have. Without confidence in their ability and a belief in their value to the team, you'll often find players dealing with a diminishing love for the game, which is the path to burnout. If it's not enjoyable and they aren't valued, they won't stick around.

What are tryouts for?

So what's the purpose of tryouts. The simple answer is that tryouts are designed to fit players with the appropriate level of play. Through tryouts, coaches and directors of coaching can place players from the same age group in direct competition to determine who fits best on which team.

Don't take this to mean that tryouts are the lone, or even the most important, aspect of player placement. For some reason, some players can just flip a switch and have a great showing at tryouts. It's the coach's duty to look beyond the two or three days of tryout sessions and look at what the player has done the previous year or two. If a player's rated near the bottom of their team the previous season, they should not move up even if they have a great showing at tryouts. From a coach's perspective, we already have a pretty good idea of what the team should look like. Having observed the players in previous seasons, we're aware of which players have shown tremendous growth, become top players on their teams, and dominated at their specific level of play. Leaving those players at the same level for the following year can only hurt their development. Those are the players who need a challenge and deserve to move up to the next team, even if their tryout showing is poor.

Ultimately, tryouts are a means of examining the fringe players and those who are new to the club. If I've watched Katie develop over the previous three seasons, I don't need a two-day tryout event to determine her level of play. I already know. But this new girl, Elizabeth, I know nothing about her and need to spend some time assessing her quality to see where she fits into the club. I also need to see how she compares to players in a similar position.

An individual team's roster needs are known by the coach and so he'll look to fill whatever needs he has on the roster. In addition to looking at the new players, he also needs to look at those fringe players from the team below to determine if they fill his current side's needs. He'll also have to see if one of those players has developed at such an exceptional rate that he needs to make the move to a higher level of play. Those are the coach's responsibilities during tryouts.

In our club, we're basically doing away with tryouts for people who have been in our system. What would happen is we watched these kids play all year long, then we come to the tryout piece and there are 300 kids trying out for these teams thinking, "I'll work really hard for three nights, as hard as I can, but where do I fall?"

It is the most stressful process within the game. We've tried to move away from that by having lots of depth charts, lots of conversations in where you are within a team, know if there's really a reality of whether you can move up or down, and trying to soften that blow or give some encouragement in those areas.

Most parents are pretty realistic about where their child is. If you're on a team and you know you're not always in the starting 11, maybe coming off the bench or you're not getting as much time, there's more of a chance that

> you may not make that team the next year. So managing the expectations is critical.
>
> How you approach it with your child is to not get them so hyped up that "Oh, if you don't make it here, you're not going to be good, you're not going to make the team..." Instead, help them try to relax, tell them to play their best, it's all going to be alright once it's over. It's such a harsh part of the game and for young players it's terrible.
>
> -Gary Buete

Do coaches show bias? Positional, character, playing style, and family considerations

Based on the previous couple of pages, you might get the sense that coaches can show bias during tryouts. There is certainly that aspect and coaches will occasionally make decisions that seem…shall we say…political in nature. We won't deny it, these picks do happen from time to time and there's not much you can do about it, which is an unfortunate part of dealing with human beings. Ideally, clubs will take a more objective look and look to limit these political decisions.

For the most part, you will find that coaches simply want the best players available. You may or may not agree with their selection, but remember that each coach sees the game in a slightly different way. One player may have qualities that are unappreciated by one coach but seen as necessary by another. These situations are tough to experience, but it is necessary to remember that each coach is trying to find players that can fit their philosophical or tactical demands.

Plus, you will recall, that if a player who's on the fringe of one team or another is either unreliable in their practice attendance, a bit of a nuisance within the team, or if there is a history of issues with the parents, that's another area where the coaches could go in another direction.

It's a tough reality but simply the way it is. Coaches construct teams for cohesion and performance. We want players who will buy into the program and fully commit to the process. Players or families that struggle in these regards will often face the consequences at the following season's tryouts.

Is bias okay?

Simply put, in most cases, bias is not okay.

But bias is different from preference, so, before you contact the club or a coach, you will want to take some time to let the situation diffuse and clear your head. When arguing that there's a case of bias in player selection, you're saying there was prejudice directed against your child, which is a very serious concern. It doesn't happen often, but there are certainly cases of it.

In the vast majority of cases, we're talking about a matter of preference. That's when the coach might prefer a certain type of player, certain skill sets, or a very specific fit for a position of need.

Here are some of the preferences you'll see from coaches:

1. Some prefer the big, fast, strong athletes
2. Others prioritize highly technical players
3. Another coach might prefer players with high soccer IQs

Ideally, players will offer a nice blend of those three qualities, as well as an excellent psychological profile, but coaches do have certain preferences and look for players who fit that mold.

At what point does advocating make sense?

This is a tricky topic. On the one hand, clubs hear an abundance of complaints during and after the tryout process, most of which is utterly ridiculous and promptly ignored. Everyone wants to move up to the next team or, for players near the bottom of the roster ranking, keep their spot. In some cases, parents develop a reputation with the club, submitting annual complaints in the build-up to tryouts and then again during tryouts.

Let's be honest, in most cases, it's a tool for manipulating an unearned roster spot. As parents, we do tend to look at our kids through rose-colored glasses, so we're not always seeing the same picture as coaches and directors. We probably aren't seeing the same thing as others in the parent group either.

Before contacting the club to file a complaint or advocate for your child, here are a few things to ask yourself.

1. Over the course of the previous season, did my child's teammates rely on her an inordinate amount?
2. Was my child a mainstay in the starting lineup and someone they coach built the tactics around?
3. If my child is a forward, was she the leading goal scorer on the team? If a midfielder, did he tend to receive and send more passes than any of the other midfielders and direct play? If a defender, when opponents did score, how often was my child involved in the goals his team conceded? If a goalie, how many times in a game did my child make saves that drew rousing reactions from the crowd and how many mistakes led to goals?

In the end, only a few players have a chance to move up a team per season. Doing the math, if your child either frequently or even occasionally started the game on the bench, odds are they should not be promoted. If your child was a consistent starter, but more of a role player on the team, promotion to the next level is largely dependent on the needs of that next team. Finally, if your child was an absolute standout, even to the degree that her teammates, the coach, and the majority of the parent group wanted the ball at her feet as often as possible, then your kid has positioned herself for a chance to play at the next level.

We always tell our players, before you tell us you want to move up, tell us who on that next team you should replace. If you're good enough to move up to the next team, that means you're good enough to send somebody down to take your spot on your current team. The conversation tends to get a little quieter then.

Here are the final takes on the topic.

Before advocating on behalf of your child, take some time to sit back and think about their status within the team. Unless it's absolutely clear that your child was head and shoulders above 90% of the team and an absolute force during games, we recommend holding off on that email. Remember, demanding a promotion when it isn't earned can only hurt your child's chances in the future. There are a lot of parents with delusions of grandeur. Don't be one of them.

If your child is in the top three or four players on the team, he'll still have to fight for promotion at tryouts, showing that he's worthy of the spot on that next team, but he's already done the heavy lifting with his excellent play the previous season. If you do feel the need to approach the club, it's best to contact the director of coaching for the age group in a respectful manner.

Even better, this is another opportunity for your child to learn how to advocate for themselves. We wouldn't recommend advocating at tryouts or immediately after team selection. Better yet, your child should have a running dialog with her coach to see where she can improve and what it takes to reach the next level. Think of it this way, if your player is waiting until tryouts to show a desire to either earn a promotion or to keep her spot on the current team, she's waiting too long. Understand that player development is a process. Those who show excellent commitment and progression over the course of the year are more likely to earn a favorable placement at tryouts. Encourage dialogue. Empower your child to take charge of their development and use the coaches as an accountability partner. In our experience, it's these players who become key figures within their team and earn promotion.

Summary

1. No demographic enjoys the tryout process, but it's part of the youth soccer experience, so it's best to enter with a realistic assessment of placement and understanding in the outcome.

2. The purpose of tryouts is simple, to place players at an appropriate level of play. That said, human beings with preferences are responsible for selecting the players best suited to their approach.

3. Before hitting send on that email complaint or dialing a phone number to complain about the tryout results, run through the questions in this chapter and think about whether or not the call is justified. If a comparable player was selected before your child, communication is unwarranted. If there's a clear case of one player being superior to the other, and we're talking about it not being close based on the previous season's production, then a respectful conversation is reasonable. At the very least, it helps to know why a lesser player was given the spot and what your child should work on in the upcoming year.

Practice & Tactical Periodization

Practice, you wanna talk about practice?

Well good, so do we.

It's a dynamic, multifaceted topic. You can look at it from the parents, players, coaches, or club's angle. The challenge here is to tie in each of those aspects to the distinct parts of the practice.

Before arriving – The Mental Approach and Deliberate Focus

First, from a player's perspective, we have that window before practice begins. For most, this is just the car ride to the field, but we recommend expanding it to packing the bag and gathering equipment at home.

Before arriving at the field, players should start mentally preparing for the session. Granted, this is easier with a middle school or high school-aged player than an elementary school-aged child, so your level of involvement as a parent will depend on the age and maturity of your child.

If your child is a U12, maybe U13, or younger, you can play an important role in their practice preparation. The goal here is to encourage deliberate practice. Recall the 10,000-hour rule for skill mastery. The endpoint isn't the number of hours. The ultimate objective of that rule is a deliberate approach to skill acquisition through experience. When your young player is packing their soccer bag or sitting in the car on the drive to practice, feel free to ask them what part of their game they want to improve that day. Have they identified one weakness that they can really focus on during practice? If so, try and get them to talk about what they'd like to improve and then briefly follow up after practice.

Keep in mind that their plan might not coincide with the practice objectives. If the goal is to improve their shooting, which, let's face it, that's every young player's goal, the coach focusing on building out of the back might limit their attempts to goal. Depending on your knowledge level, you could look to encourage more universal topics. Sure, if the opportunity to improve their shooting is there, go for it. Can they work on their first touch? What about the way they identify and move into space? Are they open to working on their communication with teammates, showing better focus during the team huddles, or improving their relationship with a teammate? Those are all reasonable points of emphasis at practices.

As kids progress to middle school age, the hope is that they'll go to practice with an objective in mind, all without your prodding. We want to teach our kids to see the opportunity in the ordinary. Sure, it's just one practice, but with this one practice, there's an opportunity to get 1% better. Teaching kids to value that small, incremental improvement is such an important skill. By the time they're driving themselves to and from practices and games, you'll see the impact of those early conversations.

Fair warning, you don't want to be overbearing. As you talk to your child, you want to be as concise as possible. If you can keep it to a single question and maybe a couple of follow-ups, you are in great shape. As best possible, let your child take the lead in their developmental process. If you want to raise a self-starter, both in soccer and life, give them an opportunity to direct their focus. Trust us, it's tough. There's always a temptation to say a little bit more, to give a little more guidance, and pull them away from the path they've determined to the one that we know will streamline the process.

Letting the kids have that final say, then letting them learn from that situation is a valuable tool. If your child can analyze their decisions and thoroughly assess what they've done well and where they went wrong, you're increasing the likelihood that they'll make those same adjustments later on in life. Let them fail now while the stakes are low. Once they've experienced and worked their way out of enough failures, they'll be unstoppable.

Arrival

We'll keep this portion of the chapter short and sweet. Get to practice 10 or 15 minutes early. On the girls' side, this is such an important bonding moment for the kids. They will willingly arrive 10 or 15 minutes early just so they can spend some time with their friends and talk. Building those friendships and developing the social culture at the team is so important.

For the guys, we guarantee that the first thing they'll do once their cleats are on is that they'll grab a ball and either shoot on goal or start another kind of competition, like a rondo. One of Scott's favorite teams was a U18 boys group. Every single player arrived at practice at least 15 minutes early. Some of the guys would show up 30 to 45 minutes early. They didn't sit around and talk. The reason they showed up at practice early was that they love the competition of rondos (keep away) and crossbar challenges. The competition started early and it carried on throughout the 90-minute session. They loved competing and they showed up early to ensure they could maximize their time in competition. From a male's perspective, that's such an incredibly fun culture to be a part of.

Interaction with Teammates and Coach

Once you've sent your child to the coaches and teammates, you've done your duty. Depending on how far you live from the field or if you need to run errands, feel free to take off and do what you need to do. It's important that parents don't feel any remorse for leaving the fields or experience any pressure to stay. If you've got something to do, know that your kid will be so busy during the session that they won't even notice you're gone.

Thinking back to our own childhoods, we acted more freely when our parents weren't around. You probably felt that same way. So don't worry. Do what you need to do and know that your child will be just fine engaging in the practice of his own accord.

If you do stay, once you send little Jimmy out to his teammates, that needs to be your last interaction for the next hour and a half, or however long your training session is. While the kids are at play, let them focus on the task at hand.

You'll know if your presence serves as more of a distraction than a supporting role if you're speaking to your child during the session or if your child is continuously looking at you instead of engaging in the exercises. Remember, this is a time for him to engage his teammates and coach, working through the problems presented in the exercises. Focus must remain fixed on the task at hand for development to occur. This can be really tough at the younger age groups. The occasional wave with the big grin on your 7 or 8-year old's face is fine, but you do want to make sure that their attention is almost exclusively on the training session.

Within the practice itself, each coach has their own style. Some are very strict, even to the degree that they don't like to see players smiling or laughing during the practice as a way of targeting focus. Others are a little bit looser, interacting with the players between exercises, laughing and joking with them to build the relationship. That's all specific to the coach and you'll see how each coach sets the tone of the practice through their own personality.

Regardless of the coach's personality, you do want to see focus during the quick team huddles and lively competition during the exercises themselves.

Clean vs Chaos

If you do happen to catch a practice, you'll likely see several teams on the field at the same time. As you look from one practice to the other, you'll probably find sessions with different objectives in play, even within the same club.

The two contrasting styles you'll most often see are clean and controlled exercises, often in the form of passing patterns or line drills, which are in contrast to the seemingly more chaotic exercises of a game-led model. You will find coaches who use a little bit of each methodology, maybe leaning more heavily towards small-sided or larger number games, but also incorporating some kind of a static exercise at the beginning of practice. Some of the more static exercises, such as ball manipulation or ball-striking activities can be very important at the younger age groups. It slows the players down and focuses their attention on just the action itself. Ideally, the next game will force them to incorporate the new skill they've just learned.

Analyzing the difference between clean vs chaotic methodologies, your initial response is probably to prefer cleaner exercises. Right off the bat, it just sounds better and more appropriate.

We won't spend too much time on the difference between the two pedagogies in this book, but, in general, the major difference between the two is context.

In cleaner exercises, such as passing lines, ball manipulation exercises, or striking technique training, the elements that play are ball manipulation and fitness. In some passing patterns, you might get a little bit of the tactical aspect, but those patterns are rarely carried out in games.

The reason is that games are dynamic. If you're interested in further study, we highly recommend podcasts, articles, and books on ecological dynamics. That's one of the hot theories in the coaching world. The basic idea is that soccer is a game in flux. The information is inherently dynamic, with reference points changing at every single moment in the game. If you have a preconceived pattern that you want the ball to follow, well guess what, you've got opponents to work around. They won't give you that specific pattern quite as easily as you'd like or as you saw in practice.

The chaotic approach is designed to deliver the ecological dynamics of the game within training sessions. Context is king. Within the chaotic methodology, players are working on the technical, tactical (be it small numbers or big picture), physical, and psychological demands of the game. It's a holistic approach that enhances each player's soccer IQ while developing a more confident player on the ball. It normalizes pressure from defenders, which leads to a more focused and intelligent approach on the field.

Johan Cruyff, the great Dutch player and coach who gave us Total Football, told his players that, "technique was not being able to juggle a ball 1,000 times. Anyone can do that by practicing. Then you can work in the circus. Technique is passing the ball with one touch, with the right speed, at the right foot of your teammate." When we talk about developing a player's technique, that's what we want. Game context is at the heart of that description. It's finding the right strike or the right action for the given scenario. A player is technical if they can meet the demands of the game on a routine basis.

That's a point John Kerr referenced as well, relaying the way his dad, John Kerr Sr. who played internationally for Canada, spoke of technique: "Ultimately, he talked about it [technique] like a set of golf clubs, that you need to have clubs if you're going to be in a sand trap when you need to chip the ball up or when you need to drive it over distance with more accuracy you use a three or four iron. If you really want to drive the ball and smack it from distance, use a driver." Each context presents its own set of demands. A game-led approach, such as play-practice-play, the preferred model of US Soccer, delivers those situational variabilities.

Don't take this as attacking coaches that use clean, static exercises. A coach can also run a game model session poorly. The types of exercises play a big role in the quality of the session, but so does the feedback from the coach.

> **I think too much of our youth soccer culture is over-coaching, where you're just sitting there and the coach is telling you what to do every single second of the game and you lose your love of the ball and love of the game.**
>
> **-Anson Dorrance**

One common misconception is that coaches who are always talking or yelling at the kids are more effective in drilling information into the minds of their players. Here in the USA, ask anyone to describe their ideal coach and, more often than not, you'll hear them give a description of their favorite NFL coach. They love an aggressive and vocal coach.

I think we've all seen coaches who fit that model out on the soccer field with their U12 girls. Quite frankly, it's devastating to watch. Fear is a motivator, but it's neither a good one nor does it help the learning process. Kids are neither adults nor professionals, so expecting them to handle verbal and psychological abuse from someone twice their size is absurd. Quite frankly, you and I wouldn't tolerate that type of talk directed against us, so why should we expect that from the kids?

Before we wrap up this chapter, it's important to take note of some of the more successful soccer cultures in the world. In countries like Portugal and Spain, coaches are often reprimanded for talking too much, for giving too many instructions, and refusing to let players solve their own problems. When you look at the quality of players they've produced in the past couple of decades, it's hard to argue against the approach.

Essentially, when coaches, parents, or teachers are simply giving the kids the answers or simplifying the conundrum, we're not training our kids how to solve the problem. Rather we're letting them get the simplified answer right, dumbing down the problem so that everyone feels accomplished. While there is some value in success, after all, the devastation of continued failure doesn't help anyone, the challenge for coaches, parents, and teachers is to ask the right questions. We don't want to solve the problem for the kids. Rather, when they get stuck, we want to ask the questions that get their minds back on track.

Again, each coach will have a different style. Some are more vocal, some are more reserved, and some are very balanced. As parents, our priority is to see that our children are challenged and given the opportunity to solve those challenges. A successful practice offers that opportunity to the kids.

So, whether your child's coach takes a cleaner or more chaotic approach, is more vocal or less so, move beyond the noise of the session and try to look at it on a meta-level. Ask, "is this session challenging my kid and am I seeing them gradually solve the little issues that arise?" If those elements are in place, kick back and relax with the confidence that your child is on the right track.

Play-practice-play, which I think is really successful, is learning by doing, problem-solving, and challenging players with questions, like, 'so why did this happen?' Humility and understanding are really important

because I can yell at you all I want, but if you don't know what I'm saying or contextually what that means, it means nothing. I'm just going to break you down and you're going to turn your attitude against me, you're going to shut down mentally, you're going to think I'm picking on you, or a number of other negative reactions. I'm a big supporter of play-practice-play, of just letting them figure it out in games.

You see a lot of these coaches on game days standing on the edge of their technical box, screaming at kids in the game. If you feel the need to do that as the coach at a youth level, especially pre-U17, you've done something wrong. It's too late. Your intentions are wrong because you're playing to get a result. There's a difference between being competitive while playing to win and playing only to win.

-Heath Pearce
Former US International and Current Chief Creative Officer at For Soccer Ventures

Summary

1. Players who enter training sessions with a clear personal object, such as improving their first touch, are likely to get more out of practice and show better focus.
2. Arriving early helps the kids fill their social and competitive needs. Once the kids are with their coach and teammates, let them go. Feel free to kick back and watch the session, run some errands, and do something for yourself during your free time.
3. Clean vs chaos is a big talking point in the coaching world. Though we prefer some chaos, which maintains a higher level of fidelity to the game, remember that great coaches can run quality clean sessions and bad coaches can ruin a game-centric approach.

Game Day Communicating

Game days are special. We have participated as players, referees, coaches, and parents. Each role views the day differently. I thought I would share each perspective so we can get a whole view of reality.

Parents' Perspective

Game days are special. We rearrange our life and social schedule around the weekend soccer matches. When we drive to the game, I'll give my player last-minute instructions in order to win. When we get to the fields, the players run off to warm up with their team. We watch the end of the previous match with an atmosphere of parents cheering and yelling at them for the win. We sit with our favorite friends (or at least the parents of the favorite friend of our kid).

The game dramedy begins. We cheer for the players; we give them advice loudly; we make comments to the referees. When the game gets intense, we cheer and yell even more with an occasional snarky comment to the other team's players or parents. We complain about our coach sometimes. We yell at the referee for missing calls. Winning is paramount where intensity can reach bloodsport level at the Colosseum on Sundays. When we drive home, we debrief the game and we instruct our kids what they should and shouldn't have done. The next day we get up and do it all over again.

Youth Referee Perspective

Game days are special. I loved them as a player. I want to give back to the community and make a few bucks even though I could make more flipping burgers. My significant other and family wants me to stop so I can spend more time with them. But, I love the atmosphere of the match. I like making decisions on the spot. During a game, I will make ~50 decisions. I try hard to make them correctly, but I am wrong sometimes. I try to learn from those mistakes. I will never change a call because a coach or parent yells at me. That questions my authority. The truth is that I will always choose to be wrong once rather than be perceived as wishy-washy and weak. I don't like when parents yell at me; they often don't really know the rules. I really don't like when the players yell at me. They often don't know the rules. There is no way for them to be objective in the heat of the moment. I really don't like having to get parents thrown off the pitch. Or when parents follow me to the car. I get the sense that their anger may be from something else in their life than a call on their player. Winning is great but isn't youth soccer about helping kids develop first and foremost?

Coach Perspective

Gamedays are special. I love working with kids during the week. Games validate if the players get the principles and tactics trained during the week. I get great satisfaction helping individual players. My significant other and family tell me that I should find work where I can earn more income with less criticism or spend more time with them. But, I love what I do. During games, I usually have the players focus on 2-3 things and then just play the game. Depending on the level, I am active in giving instructions. Other times, it's best to wait until halftime, after the game, or at practice. I like when parents cheer for their players. I get annoyed when they instruct the players on what to do. I have given a plan out to the kids and the parents want to supersede the plan with what they think works.

I know that the primary goal is to help players develop. But, the parents want to win; the club wants to win; I want to be able to tell the other coaches around the water cooler that we won. The truth is fewer than half the teams are going to win over a weekend given ties. Deep down I want the kids to be better players and humans. I feel the pressure of winning even though it can run counter to their player's development.

I don't like when parents yell at me during games. I look bad in front of kids and parents. Oftentimes, they don't really know the modern game even though they may have played. Their kids feel miserable. The truth is that these exchanges hurt their kids' chances. I like when parents set up a call or chat during the week once there is some perspective gained.

Players

Gamedays are special. I just want to play. I want to win. I want to hang out with my teammates. Games are stressful. My parents tell me how to play before a game. Coach tells me how to play before, during, and after the game. Parents are yelling at me to do things when everything is going a million miles an hour. The truth is I tune out a lot of what they are yelling because it is too much information. I see how parents think that the coach or the referee doesn't know what they are doing. Everyone wants us to win. My teammates and the other team players sense this ultimate need to win. Though I get told what I did well, I remember what I did wrong on the car ride home. I just want to play.

BEST PRACTICES

Gamedays are amazing. Based on our experiences, players do best when they are in the flow, namely, they are in the moment playing the game. The main goal should be how my player is getting better this week rather than last. No one is really going to remember if a game was won or lost. We are all wired to want to win. Development is a process. Let's wait until college, pros, or World Cups before winning becomes the primary goal.

We had to realize that it is about the kids playing, not about us. We had the chance to play. It's their turn and will likely be very different from our own. The game has changed so much in the last few years. Here is what we have found to be effective.

Chris's Advice on…
Communicating with Players

Pregame: If I give advice before a game, I have them be mindful of 1-2 easy things to execute. For example, look around yourself before you receive the ball. I ask my player what does the coach want them to focus on during the game.

During game: I generally don't communicate with my player during the game. There is so much stressful stimulus going on that they will likely forget within a few minutes. I may cheer positively but kids can sense insincerity, especially of their parents. The reality is that most players don't hear or remember much from what is being yelled by the sidelines. There is already too much stimulus.

Postgame: I ask them what their take was on the game. Then, I ask what the coach thought. I do my best to wait until they ask what I thought of the game. I adjust my response based on what their take and the coach's take was. I ask what they learned from the game. Finally, I tell them to enjoy the positive moments, crystallize key learnings, and forget about the rest.

Communicating with Referees

I never communicate with refs. I admit I break that rule occasionally when the linesperson doesn't keep up with the last defender and misses the offsides call. You will hear me rarely yell offsides. No ref has ever changed any other call in my 35 years in the sport. I didn't when I was a licensed referee. I don't like when they get a couple of calls wrong but the truth is they are underpaid, underappreciated, and someone else's daughter or son.

Communicating with Coaches

I never communicate with coaches on game day, except to commiserate or congratulate them. If you want to communicate with them, wait until another day when heads are clearer.

Communicating with Parents

I have friendly chats with teammates' parents. I don't give false compliments because people know when it's false. I only give advice when I am asked.

I never communicate with other team's parents unless it's a friendly Q&A. I imagine that they love their kids as much as you love yours. They may be loud and passionate, but that may be a disservice to their players.

Summary

1. Parents, referees, coaches, and players all go into game days with their own sets of perspectives and objectives. As parents and coaches, a player-centered approach will yield

the greatest fruit.

2. Going into game days with a plan is key. Chris's best practices guideline is a great model for engaging at all levels.

3. As parents, we can work towards a club or team-wide standard of values and model our game day approaches off of those core values. Team managers can play an important role in enforcing the parents' sideline's core values and terms of engagement, but there has to be support and buy-in from most of the group. Whether you like the parent group or not, you're stuck with them for at least a season. How can you spearhead a positive relationship with the other families and the youth soccer experience as a whole? A discussion of and adherence to core values on the sidelines is a great place to start, then dig deeper by building a community.

Maintaining Sanity on Game Days

Quick! Think back to your childhood. What are the first thoughts that come to mind during your youth sports days?

Were your first thoughts about moments of extreme success or failure?

We tend to hold on to those more extreme, less common accomplishments or failures. They're easy enough to remember because of their significance or infrequency. In all likelihood, your first thoughts about your own experience were attached to one of those two types of moments.

Now dig a little deeper.

Beyond those easily recollected memories, what are some of the more general thoughts and feelings you experienced?

Yes, that was a long time ago for most of us, but take this moment to dig a little deeper and pull some of those old experiences to the surface.

You might remember loving the competitiveness of the game and practice environments. Maybe you were on the other side of the spectrum and had a fear of making mistakes. We've coached some players who, at least initially, didn't even want the ball at their feet. Such was their fear of making mistakes.

Some of us will recall really supportive coaches and parent groups who were very encouraging and diffused the natural pressure that's built into competition. But we'll all likely recall the coach or parents whose wild exclamations simply made the game tenser.

You know the saying, some people live vicariously through their children.

Behind the intense presence of some coaches and parents is the joy or success that they've experienced as kids or in adulthood. They want the kids to share in that joy, to know what it's like to win tournaments, to score big goals. In most cases, we find that the intention is good even if the interaction itself tends to build pressure rather than relieve it.

You'll also find some coaches or parents whose approach is laden with anxiety. There are a couple of possible influences here. First, and this one is typically more prevalent on the parent side, is that they don't want their kids to experience the heartbreak of loss or failure. No one wants bad things to come upon their children and, let's face it, it does pain us to see our kids suffer, so that's one of the motivating causes for this type of interaction.

Secondly, and this one can go to either the parents or the coaches but I find it's more common with the latter, is that anxiety builds when we see the kid's performance as an extension of our influence. If our child or a team has lost, some personalize it to think it's their fault and a sign of their weakness and ability. That's a tremendous burden and one that is easily transmitted to the kids. We've noticed that some of the most anxious players tend to have at least one parent who was a very successful youth or collegiate athlete. There's a lot to live up to and that burden is placed on the kids.

So how can we reshape our approach to games in a way that brings the best out of our kids?

> **We come from these U.S. traditional sports, which are just a "put your foot on their throat" type of thing and play to win. I think there is too much of an emphasis on winning and they don't understand playing to learn and develop can still come with winning. It could still be winning. You can still do it this way, but it's not about getting points to get to the next tournament. It's not about being nationally ranked. It's not about that even at the highest level or the most recreational levels. There's a cultural problem with allowing kids to learn on the job, allowing them to be out there and express themselves and figure things out.**

There was a study called the Swag Study from Adidas that they did a couple of years ago of the Elite Soccer Program kids. The best 60 kids in the country are part of the ESP camp. Most of these kids are MLS Academy kids, the top of the food chain of soccer players. One of the top two traits that they all shared at 16, 17 years old - our best kids in the country, our future pros - is fear. Fear of making mistakes, fear of letting the team down, fear of losing your starting position, fear of not playing, fear of getting yelled at.

We've sucked all the creativity out of these kids, because the emphasis is put on, "okay, it's a good idea to try that, but maybe you just kick it in the goal because then we win." It was really alarming to read that study. These are the elite players. I could see this in kids in the community where they live in their little bubble, they want to win the local tournament, and the parents are on their backs.

These are the top players. These are the ones that have broken out of that level and they're still fearful of what it means to make mistakes…and that is a major problem.

-Heath Pearce

Failure is okay

First, we can let them know that mistakes and failures are okay. It's not the end of the world to lose the championship game of a tournament. It will sting, hopefully far more for the players than the parents or coaches, but even this setback can be a source of development and motivation.

If you're like us, you hated losing as a kid. Maybe even to the point where significant losses brought on new training regimens. No one enjoys a loss, but losing in vain is the greatest failure of all.

You see, with each loss, the spotlight shines brightly on weaknesses.

It's the greatest teacher. The feedback is immediate, and we know exactly what we can do, both individually and collectively, to make progress. Losses are only a failure if they don't lead to action, to correction. If a player gets in the habit of scrutinizing their own performance, noting what they could have done better and what they have done well, then they're showing a mature and growth-oriented approach to their personal development.

Cheering vs Directing

There's a huge distinction to make here. Sidelines at soccer games can get pretty crazy. We've seen cases where close to 200 friends and family members gathered around a U8 field to cheer on their five aside players. The scene was pro-game supporters section crazy! That's a pretty uncommon circumstance and maybe something you'll find only at the very youngest age groups when everyone wants to see their tiny tot playing locally, but it does remind us that we are setting an environment for the kids to play.

Remember that you've paid for coaching. As our kids run out onto the field, they're not just conducting individual actions. After a week, or even a season, of training, they enter the playing field as part of a network, connecting their actions to those of their teammates. That's what makes for a successful team and allows for the success of individual players.

So, if the game is underway, know that the players love it when the parents' sideline cheers. What we mean here is that we're providing a reaction to an event that has already occurred. Maybe a goal was scored, a shot taken, a beautiful pass completed, or just a strong defensive effort. Those are things we want to praise. And by all means, do it. The kids love it and coaches appreciate the encouragement for the kids.

Directing is entirely different. What we mean by directing is that a play is either in the process of happening or it's about to happen and instructions are coming from the sideline. If you're telling the kids which actions to undertake, that's when you're directing the child's play.

There are a few points to make here. First, there's a pretty good chance they're not going to hear you. Some kids do manage to pick out their own parents' voices throughout the game, but there are so many other things that they're focusing on that outside voices can go unnoticed, making the directions a waste of breath.

Secondly, there is a lot of information running through their minds. They're not only trying to decide on which action to take, but they're also absorbing communication from teammates as well. The information demands from the field itself can be so overwhelming that instructions from the sideline only complicate the matter, slowing down the decision-making process. In most cases, even a half-second delay in the decision can lead to a turnover. Players absolutely need that mental space to intellectually engage the game and take action.

Third, telling the kids to "score a goal" or "pass it" is comparable to yelling at the TV to tell Cristiano Ronaldo to score a goal. That's what he wants to do. Me telling him to go score a goal is entirely unnecessary. At least from one side of the TV, my yelling isn't serving as a distraction. Early on in our coaching careers, we realized that screaming "shoot" as the player was shooting was not only unnecessary, but a distraction. We wish we had the stats but we're going to guess that the players shanked the shot more often than they scored a goal when we yelled some needless type of information to them.

Finally, there's the reminder that the player's actions are not in isolation. You might wonder why a kid isn't switching the point of attack sooner or playing long to the fast forward up top, but, in all likelihood, their actions are tying into a week's worth of practices and a season of development. As the season progresses, coaches structure the training sessions to hit on different technical and tactical actions. If one week they're building out of the back at practice, coaches want to see those exercises and ideas in use at games. So, yes, that tall fast forward who has a lot of success running past backlines is wide open and it is probably the easiest way to score a goal, but we have to look at the bigger picture. That's not requiring much of the entire team nor looking after the long-term development of the players. Implementing the ideas from practice inherently prioritizes long-term development. It's the ideas and progression in playing style that shows growth, not necessarily the wins. The surface-level interpretation is certainly the easiest, but the bigger picture is far more important.

If it seems like we've beaten you up a little bit in this section, please know that's not the intention. We're parents ourselves. We'd love to get wrapped up in the game and we do have to fight off the urge to direct the players' actions. It's even more difficult from a coach's perspective. However, if Lionel Messi and Luis Suárez can sit at Barcelona youth games and patiently watch their kids make mistakes and solve problems, then I suppose our limited soccer geniuses should as well. We want our kids to succeed, but if that short-term success comes at the expense of long-term development, we've cheapened the developmental process and limited our children's ceiling.

Interaction with referees

He'll never forget it. Early on a Saturday morning, Scott's nephew, who at the time was 7 years old, was playing in a local U8 rec basketball league. It was a tense game, a real nail-biter. Late in the game, the teams were locked in a tie, a blistering 12-12 game. And then, it happened. One of the U8 players had traveled. The dreaded U8 travel! And you know what, no call from the referee. Outrageous! The fans in the stand lost it. 50 adults started screaming at the referee, the echoes reverberated across the gym, creating a hostile environment to voice their displeasure with his egregious decision. The injustice was incredible.

If only those 50 people had taken a step back to remember that, 1) it was a U8 game and 2) the referees had shown some leniency towards traveling all game, because 3) the kids were U8s and 4) there's no need to treat a youth referee like he's officiating a professional game.

Look, we've all had our frustrations with the referees. The two of us are guilty as well, even in the way we conduct our conversations with the referees. Your fun fact for the day is that Scott has picked up more yellow cards as a coach than he ever did as a player, that despite being a hard-nosed defensive midfielder who loved to put in a strong tackle.

We all want to stand up for our kids and ensure the opponents are not taking cheap shots at them or making contact that can lead to injuries. We also want a fair game. At times, referees do show bias.

In those situations, the best advice we can give is to trust the coach to handle it. It's her duty first and foremost to stand up for the kids and ensure that the game is officiated fairly and consistently. If a conversation with the ref is necessary, they are typically open to conversations with the captains of each team and the coaches, not the parents. In fact, screaming from the parents' sideline will only get you kicked out. The referees then make a note of the ejection in their match report, which is sent to the state association, then to the club, the director of coaching, and the coach, who will typically have to have a conversation with you about your game conduct. It's a long-drawn-out process and not enjoyable for anyone. Let the coaches handle confrontations.

This is especially important if you are still new to the Laws of the Game and what is fair contact vs unfair. Over the years, we've seen a lot of parents outraged by fair challenges. Sure, the contact was hard and the kid hit the ground hard, but that's not enough to make it a foul. Some of our best challenges as players sent the opponents flying, but, because of the context of those situations and the type of contact we had on the play, they were fair tackles. Soccer's a physical, contact sport. We have to allow for it and not take offense when that contact goes against our teams.

Further, the best piece of advice that I've received on the topic is that if we want to show outrage when our team has been fouled, then we should do the exact same thing when our kids foul the opponents. If contact or hard challenges are that egregious, then the response should go both ways.

In the end, know that fouls are going to happen, that hard tackles are a part of the game, and that, if necessary, the coach or captain will handle the situation by talking to the referees.

The car ride home

This is a big one. What's your plan for the car ride home?

Do you ask the kids for a full analysis of the game? Do you give a full analysis of the game yourself? Is it a time to praise, to berate, or to investigate?

In the last chapter, you saw how Chris used the car ride home as a means of letting the player process the game and use the trip home as a way to release some of their immediate thoughts. No parental opinions, just open-ended questions the kids can run with…if they want.

The best advice Scott's received on the topic came from a collegiate coach. John Keating, coach of the Belmont Abbey College men's soccer team wrote an excellent letter to his former club's parent group, explaining exactly how he approaches the car rides home with his four kids.

The key takeaway? Let them be.

Remember, they've just played a full game, they're mentally and physically exhausted, and they're still trying to process what's happened. In all likelihood, they're not ready to launch into a detailed discussion about the game. They may need some time to run scenarios back in their mind and consider where they've done well and what they could improve, both on an individual and team basis.

Taking a player-led approach allows them to set the tone and timing, which, in turn, will lead to a more fruitful conversation. If your goal is to open the lines of communication and give your child a chance to relay their thoughts about the game, let them do it on their time.

Rush the conversation or force them to speak about the game immediately after it has ended you'll not only have a lousy conversation, but you're likely to see your child start drifting further from those talks. The toll may even move beyond soccer and into other areas of your child's life.

There's a time to initiate the conversation and a time to challenge them, but the key is in the timing itself. As a general philosophy, you'll end up with a better relationship and have more productive conversations if you give your child time to process the game. Keep your questions simple and open. When your child is ready for a conversation, guided questions will help them work out their thoughts, especially if there's a problem they want to solve. Don't go into the conversation looking to create problems for them. Just show an openness to what they're experiencing. If you're in a position to give advice, take it, but we have to make sure we're not force-feeding our kids with information they don't care to process.

> **You'll learn early on that the hardest thing to do as a parent, is to actually keep your mouth closed. Because you get into the car and you just want to say, and I've been guilty of it, "hey, why did you do this" or "why do you think the coach did that" or "what happened in this situation." And you know, even for myself, with the experience that I've had in the game, it's really hard not to try to interject my life experiences and my knowledge of the game onto the kid sitting in the backseat that just came off the field.**
>
> **But, you know, I hope I did more of the, "hey, what are you doing next", "let's go have some ice cream", "what's going on in school", to divert the attention. It's in the best interest of the kids for them to be able to separate so that they don't feel that they're playing for the parent. They're playing for themselves.**
>
> **-Skip Gilbert**
> **CEO of US Youth Soccer**

Summary

1. It's a blessing to experience failure in the small world of youth soccer. Let the kids make mistakes while the stakes are low. These early lessons can and should spur a healthy response to failure and disappointment.

2. Respect is key. The players need it as they experience the demands of the game and the referee deserves a little bit of leeway just for putting up with us crazy parents and coaches.
3. Following from Chris's advice in the previous chapter, have a plan for the car ride home. You'll get more out of it if the player is allowed to lead the conversation.

Communicating with Coaches

Communicating with coaches can be a tricky issue. Oftentimes, parents wait too long to establish a connection with the coach. The first conversation is often a brief introduction, but then months can pass before there's any additional communication. If the second conversation involves a difficult topic, this leaves the parents and coach in the position where they're virtual unknowns to each other. That can make it difficult to determine the right approach, and by "right" we mean one that leads to a productive conversation that resolves the issue at hand.

Regardless of your relationship with the coach, we've come up with some basic guidelines for the conversation.

Setting the tone for engagement

Communicating with coaches can be a tricky subject. Each coach has his own personality or preferences for social engagement, so tailoring your communication to the coach is certainly not a one-size-fits-all.

As you get to know your child's coach, you do want to get a sense of their personality, values, and response to questions or criticism. As a parent, you can and should be invested in your child's soccer and personal development, so you do have a duty to ensure your coach has the same goals in mind.

One thing to consider as you approach the coach is to determine what kind of tone you want to set. It is a coach's duty to remain professional in conversations with parents and players, but we are human beings too. We do get frustrated, defensive, and occasionally take insult to comments against us.

As you set the tone for the conversation it is again important to remember to start with the end in mind. As we tell our players, when you speak to a teammate, even if it is a criticism, the objective is to get them back on track. We want them to re-engage mentally, to see that there is an issue with a solution. Players need their teammates to know that the support is there, that they'll have their teammates back as they work towards the solution. In the end, the desired results are resolution and peak performance.

> **Chances are, at the beginning of the season, the coach is going to set the rules as to how to approach him or her. My only comment there is to follow those rules. Respect what the coach wants regarding parent interaction and use that accordingly. At times, the parents can be the greatest advocate for the coach, can be the greatest eyes for the coach, but, at some point, there's a line you don't want to cross.**
>
> **-Skip Gilbert**

If the reason for your communication is to praise or compliment the coach, have at it. In all our years in the game, the worst reaction we've seen to praise is blushing. We may or may not be guilty ourselves.

If the reason for the conversation is criticism or concern, feel free to have that conversation, but know that you'll make the most progress if the tone is calm and constructive.

48-Hour Rule

Let's dive into the specifics. At the very least, this is an unwritten rule, though many clubs actually do implement a 48-hour rule. Basically, after an event, parents should wait 48 hours to address the coach about a concern.

Scott recalls finishing a practice one day in August to see that he received an email from a parent at 6:15, 15 minutes after his practice started. The purpose of the email was to inform him that he should have held his practice in the shade rather than in the sun. It was hot and the boys were struggling with the heat, so he gave them plenty of water breaks. However, the parent still thought it important that the boys practice in the shade.

Had the parent used the 48-hour rule, she would have had time to ask herself, "is this email really necessary?" It would have given time for a follow-up thought to come to mind, like, "We do have a game this weekend and there's no tree coverage on the field, and the game is actually at a hotter time of day than the practice, so I suppose there wasn't any harm in practicing in the sun."

We promise, if there is a legitimate concern, coaches do want to address it. But give the communication 48 hours just to make sure that the topic is legitimate.

One of the reasons to allow for the 48-hour window and give some extra thought to that potential conversation is because it does ultimately benefit you to have a good relationship with the coach and club. They'll be more responsive when you do communicate with them, plus there's the added benefit for your child.

We'll be honest, community is a big part of the youth sports experience, both on the player and parent side of the game. Say for example that you're at tryouts and there's one spot left on the team. Competing for that spot are two kids of equal or near-equal talent. If there's little to nothing between the kids in terms of talent, coaches will take the personalities of the player and families into consideration. We want a cohesive team with a supportive parent group. We want the family's associated with our team to enjoy their youth soccer experience and come back the following season. If either the player or their parents would take away from that sense of community and cohesion surrounding the team, the other kid will get the spot nearly every time.

Again, you can and should advocate for your child when necessary, especially if there is a serious or valid concern. That's part of being a parent. Both of us are parents, so we know that there is a time to step in and a time to let our kids experience some obstacles or trials. It really is a matter of determining which circumstances absolutely need addressing.

We've had a lot of discussions about communicating with coaches over the years, across all sports, and it's one of those things that parents often think, because of

the financial commitment as the kids get higher and higher up in the hierarchy of the sport, that they almost are like the general manager and that they have an intrinsic right to be able to yell at, call, or text the coach every time they have a thought.

The reality is, do you do that with their math or their science teacher? Do you do that if your kid has a summer job? Are you calling their boss every day to say, "my kid should be doing this? My kid should be doing that?"

Well, if the answer to that is "no", as it should be, why are you doing that to their coach?

-Skip Gilbert

3 Step Process: Player → Coach, Parent → Coach, Parent → Director

Most clubs require coaches to meet with the parents at the beginning and end of the season. During the preseason meeting, one of the topics should be the three-step process for addressing issues with the coach.

The first step is between the player and the coach. Kids must learn to advocate for themselves. If there is something that they feel needs addressing, they should respectfully approach the coach and have a conversation. Coaches do occasionally come across as unapproachable or even intimidating to the players, but this is great practice for that conversation with the college professor or a meeting with a future boss. One of the reasons our kids play sports is to have access to this type of situation and to learn how to approach a superior, have a difficult conversation, and work towards a resolution. It's such an important life skill and one that's taught in youth sports. Even at the age of 11 or 12, kids should take the lead in emailing the coach. Parents can advise and support, but advocating for oneself is an essential skill children must embrace.

If the player's conversation with the coach leaves the issue unresolved, the next step is for you, the parent, to get involved. This is when you want to use the ideas we've discussed in the chapter. Remember, the end goal is resolution. You want this problem solved and, in most cases, so does the coach. If your child's conversation with the coach is unproductive, it is important to get some of the details of the conversation, both from your child and the coach, but do keep in mind that kids are still learning how to navigate these conversations.

Ideally, the coach will take the lead in the conversation with the player, offering guidance and working towards a resolution. If this doesn't happen, that's when your experience comes into play. You will have to fight that Mama Bear or Papa Bear feeling, which, trust us, we know that's difficult at times, but the best advice we can give is to keep a cool head and stay on point, which is finding a resolution of the issue at hand.

If, after speaking to the coach, you're unable to solve the problem, this is when you will contact the club's director of coaching for the age group or, at a smaller club, the executive director.

In most cases, it's the director of coaching you want to contact. Since it's their job to develop the coaches, working through the issue with them provides feedback on the quality of the coach and how the DOC can help him better address the situation in the future.

In all our years of coaching and parenting young soccer players, there's rarely a necessity for even the second stage of the process. If you've got a coach who is invested in developing the kids, both as soccer players and as human beings, you'll find that he's aware of how difficult it is for the kids to have the conversation and that he will work closely with them to solve the problem. Again, this is an important life skill that kids have to learn. Most coaches welcome that type of conversation, both to help the kids in the present and prepare them for the future.

What's the Objective? Start with the End in Mind

Just to hammer home the point, whether it's you or your kid having a conversation with the coach, remember that you want to go into the conversation with the end in mind. If it's a resolution with the coach that you or your child want, remember to go into that conversation with that structure and tone in place.

Over the course of your child's youth sports career, you'll find that she has coaches of varying personalities and temperaments. Having a relationship with your coach, even if it is just small talk after a game or practice, you'll learn A lot about their personality and interests.

We've had a lot of great relationships with our players' parents. We've gone to professional sporting events with them, attended graduations, and parties the families have hosted. You'll generally find that coaches are open to a positive relationship and that they do enjoy the community surrounding the team. Plus, by getting to know your coach, you get to know who she is and what she values. That's such an incredible gift as you try to gauge how the impact of their coaching fits with your child's personal development and your parenting philosophy.

Summary

1. Setting the right tone for the conversation is critical. Get that right and you're far more likely to have a productive conversation and address the issue at hand.
2. Abide by the 48-hour rule. That gives a window for emotions to settle and allow you to assess the issue with a clear head. If it's still bothering you after 48 hours, that's a sign some level of resolution is necessary. Feel free to engage in respectful dialogue at that point.
3. Remember the three-step process for addressing issues:
   Player → Coach, Parent → Coach, Parent → Director

Supplemental Training

Youth soccer often trains 3-4 times weekly in addition to 1-2 weekend matches for 6-10 months a year. For most families, this workload and investment is perfect. Players can prosper at the classic, premier, elite, ECNL, and Academy levels.

Some players want more. While they can't control their underlying physical attributes, they can improve their technical, physical, and mental game. Depending on the family's disposable income, time, and logistics, there are several types of training to consider. While this training does not guarantee a pathway to the highest level of soccer and a college pathway, it does increase the chances considerably. In the end, these types of training will help your player be the best they can be.

First, the most important consideration is that the player really wants and is excited about additional training. The player should want this training much more than their parents. Be prepared to hit the pause button if players are getting tired or feeling overcooked. Make it a policy to ask your player if they want to stop at the end of each month so they get the sense that this is a privilege, not a right. They will likely value the training even more.

Plans

Like many sports, soccer is being planned out in terms of workloads over the course of a year. An annual plan includes specific targets for the team and individual players. For example, there is a preseason where the emphasis is speed, endurance, and skills. There is a plan to peak in the Fall and Spring seasons while taking breaks in winter and summer. However, the summer may have heavier loads for building strength and speed while maintaining those during the season.

A longer-term personal plan could be created over the span of several years. There is more suitable training for younger kids than repeating what professional athletes do after years of training.

Sometimes, the training needed to improve your player now may be inconsistent with a longer horizon training program with a peak for high school or college optimization. Developing a long-term training plan requires expertise. Most importantly, parents need to get comfortable with the idea of players getting the appropriate workloads at the right time with adequate recovery. These plans are often called periodization.

Self-training

This is the easiest start point. Tom Byer, a youth soccer thought leader, thinks that training should start in the home. Leave soccer balls around the house so even the youngest of kids can dribble their way to and fro. Kicking the ball against a wall or sofa 10 minutes a day will do wonders. Buy cones, speed ladders, return net, or a goal for the yard. The most successful kids always want to be on a soccer ball. Players can find training moves on YouTube and subscribe to a large number of coaches.

> **It's not overtraining if it's self-induced and the kid derives pleasure out of playing five hours of soccer every single day. That's his enjoyment. He believes he owns his free will, his own free time, and his own fun. That's not pressure. Pressure is when you frame it in the expectations, the pressure to win, and it's all organized. That's when the kid burns out. It's not from the actual time.**
>
> **-Tom Byer**

The next level is an online structured training such as CaptainElite.com where there is a combination of online as well as in-person options. SoccerRenegade.com is another option. These programs, which range from $150-300, offer well-curated drills and offer additional segments of confidence management and the mental game.

Game film is a great educator and guide for self-training. As players watch themselves compete, they'll have concrete feedback on the things that are going well and areas that need improvement. All you need is an action camera with a high rating of frames per second. While you don't have to film every game, periodic recording is a fantastic resource for the players and offers direct insight on areas for self-training.

Pickup

Pickup soccer is a silver bullet, particularly when playing with players older and better than yours. It's hard to find these games and get in. Drive around nearby fields to find a game. For younger kids, you may have to organize a game which would start as parent/kids pick up. Keep it fun and invest in some small-sided goals and cones. For kids over 13 years old, find adult games where they would be accommodating and be a good fit. It helps if the parents also play. Again, becoming an organizer of a game helps tremendously, which is as easy as finding 8-9 players, an open field time, and using WhatsApp for communications.

On a personal note, we find playing pickup with our kids to be more enjoyable than watching them play games. It's an activity that you can enjoy together until your knees say no more and better judgment prevails.

After a month or two, you will likely see dramatic improvements in confidence and speed of play. The higher quality, faster, and bigger the pickup game, the more potential upside. Your players are also more incentivized to train more if they see a virtuous circle.

Why Girls Should Join Boys' Pick-Up Games

Your speed of play and speed of decision making is going to be transformed as a boy is sprinting at you.

But why do I want this girl to still play with girls? For her to develop her personality and become elite. She still has to be able to take the game over and, against a boys' team, she can never take the game over. They're too athletic, so you play with the girls' team. So now when you get the ball, YOU are the general. YOU are making the final pass. YOU are scoring the goals.

> Here's what's going to happen on a boys' team. You're going to learn to play very fast. You're going to learn to play the whole game at a sprint, to be very brave, because they're going to be some 50/50s and you're going to think, "I don't know whether that's worth it to me," and you're going to have to decide whether or not you're going to risk having your legs broken. So you're going to have to do things like toe-poke it and get up in the air, because the boy's going to be coming through. So that's still very good for the girl and the boys.
>
> -Anson Dorrance

Futsal

This indoor version of soccer is amazing if your player can join a league or play pickup. Think of a super-fast 5v5 game on a basketball-size court with a smaller ball that doesn't bounce as much. In many places, futsal is played in the offseason (winter) or even as a precursor to soccer. The player's touch, speed of play, and anticipation are greatly enhanced. In Spain and South America, most youth play "baby futsal" until they are 12 years old on courts before transitioning to outdoors. This is likely the big reason why these countries produce such technically capable players. There are increasingly more and more futsal tournaments around the US to support development.

Other Sports

Encourage your player to participate in other sports as long as possible. There is a great deal of science that supports that players develop to become better athletes if they play different sports in childhood. Optimizing neural pathways in the brain is the primary benefit. Obstacles to the multi-sport athlete include time constraints, club restrictions, and money. The best advice is to encourage players to engage in other sports until it is no longer feasible. In our experiences, we pushed as long as we could while being upfront with soccer coaches about what we were doing.

When I worked at US Tennis, my function there was managing director for pro tennis operations and managing the US Open, which, arguably, is the largest annual sporting event in the world.

So I'm standing at midcourt before my first US Open. Andy Roddick, one of the great American tennis players at the time, was warming up at center court and I'm with Dr. Brian Hainline, who was our Chief Medical Officer and is now the CMO of the NCAA. I asked Brian, "why are the men so far from the top five in the world?" He said, "you tell me?"

So we watched Andy and, sure, technically - forehand, backhand, overhand - was absolutely tremendous. So I said, "he should be able to play with the best of them." He said "what else?" And I looked at him and said, "he's not a world-class athlete." He goes, "bingo. The problem with Andy is that he spent his entire youth life on the tennis court, so when he runs, he runs around the tennis court. He never was able to get his muscular-skeletal system to be able to adapt to other sports, to be able to give him what he needs to get ahead."

When you look at the top four tennis players in the world at that point - Roger Federer, Andy Murray, Novak Djokovic, Rafael Nadal - they all played soccer, all ran track, they all did multiple sports. So in this country, the average sport per person is that now at 1.81 per kid, which is the lowest it's been in years. All of the studies show that the lower it gets, the more specialized that the sports get with those kids, the more harmful it is and the more burnout. You're going to get more kids who are going to be quicker to leave the sport because they just get frustrated. We want to make sure they all play as many sports as they want when they're young.

So to all parents, I would say let your kids play in as many sports as they can. If you get a coach that says your kid needs to be playing soccer 12 months a year at the age of 8, 9, 10, or 11, go somewhere else.

Realistically, sure, your kid may be that one diamond in the rough, the one in a million, that's going to make that journey to the national team. But more likely than not, your kid is going to be one of those kids that, by the time they get to 13, they're so burned out they want to move on.

So do them a favor, let them experience other sports. And if it's in their best interest, let the kids decide that soccer is for them. Let them have the passion, the commitment, and the dedication coming from them. Not coaches telling them. Not parents telling them. It's got to come from the internal. As they get into their early teen years, if they go full bore in soccer, great. Should they go into one of the other sports that are out there, good for them.

At the end of the day, as parents, we should want our kids to embrace a healthy lifestyle so that when they're our age, they're running, they're doing triathlons, or playing soccer; they're doing whatever it is that they do to be able to maintain that healthy lifestyle ethic.

-Skip Gilbert

Personal Soccer Training

This activity is fantastic if you can afford it. Even if you can't, try to be creative about bartering for services. These additional training sessions are so helpful especially if you ask the coach to provide "homework" drills between sessions. A popular alternative is to organize 3-6 players where you share coaching fees. Some clubs provide supplemental training at affordable rates. Get some recommendations, try them out, and don't be shy about making changes if it isn't working out. Most club coaches are happy to provide personal training if their club allows for it.

Before reaching out to a coach for personal training, it's important to determine what your child needs. Player development models tend to focus on four pillars:

1. Technical

2. Tactical

3. Physical

4. Psychological

In an ideal world, your player will get all four of these elements in a private training session. Even still, it's important to identify specific areas of need. For younger players or those at the lower levels of competitive club play, a heavy emphasis on technical development through ball manipulation is the best alternative. More skilled players will benefit far more from a small group session with greater technical demands (remember technique is ball mastery in game context) and advanced ball striking exercises. Adding tactical demands through small-sided games is a step up from simple ball mastery.

Tactical training doesn't happen exclusively on the playing field either. For high-level players, there's also the possibility of film study. With the guidance of a tactically competent coach, players can either have discussions or write reports about games or players. If they choose to write, the reports don't have to be very long. They can choose to write about one team's general playing style, a single aspect of the team's tactics, or even a player that's a close positional match. 400 to 500 words is more than enough to convey the most important points. In fact, coaches might prefer a shorter version, possibly giving the bullet point version of the report. It all depends on the time and preferences of the coach and the eagerness of the player.

From the psychological side, this, again, is something coaches can and should implement in their practices and personal training sessions. As parents, we want to know that our kids are learning to cope with frustration, develop a sense of resilience, take on leadership opportunities, and know how to be good sportsmen without experiencing a drop in competitiveness. Much like the physical side, players can now get training in this specific area of the game through sports psychology.

If your area does not have sports or performance psychologists, or maybe the bank account rules out that option, there are several great resources available online or through bookstores. Dan Abraham's is one of our favorite sports psychologists. He has several books, as well as his podcast, The Sports Psych Show. This is something many older players would benefit from. The books and podcast offer a unique opportunity for sports psychology and personal growth. Even if your kids aren't actively seeing a psychologist, developing their character is a top priority for us parents. They should be getting some of that at home through family life, but we also want to encourage our kids to take ownership of their personal development. Encouraging them to read performance and sports psychology books, and even listen to character development podcasts, is a great starting point.

Speed/Agility/Strength Training

The fourth pillar includes running technique, sprints, non-soccer footwork skills, injury prevention, stretching, and mostly bodyweight training. Some clubs are beginning to offer this training. There is a great deal of growth in stand-alone gyms that specialize in these services. For prepubescent youth, these exercises are great for developing neural pathways, confidence building, and creating good life habits. Little muscle formation will occur until puberty as hormones are essential for significant growth. After puberty, this training is great fuel for rapid development.

Speed training may only last for less than 10 minutes weekly with ample recovery between sprints.

Agility training could be non-ball footwork with cones and speed ladders.

Weight training is usually bodyweight exercises such as push-ups, burpees, wall sits, barbells, and kettlebells. Heavier weight exercises start at 16-17 years old under the supervision of a qualified professional. Soccer tends to reward leaner, faster muscles as opposed to bulky size.

Generally, shorter training sessions spread out over the week is more helpful. The key is not to overload the player's body too much.

Supplemental training could be the extra 10% needed to go from one level to the next. The key is to closely monitor the workloads and enthusiasm of your player. They have to want this training more than you do because it costs time and money. An important side benefit is that this training will likely develop a lifetime of healthy skills and habits.

> **I was fortunate enough, around middle school or high school, I started working out at this place called CATS, where we did a lot of speed and agility work and strength training. A key part of it is injury prevention. I think a lot of girls, as they're growing up, are prone to injury, like ACLs. Improving activation, strength, and proprioceptive awareness while girls are growing into their bodies is really important and can help prevent injuries.**
>
> **I definitely recommend focusing on that part and doing a lot of band work. If you have access to somebody who can coach you through some of these movements that could help prevent injury, that's one of the best ways to maintain your ability to play.**
>
> **-Sam Mewis**

Individual vs Small Group

In our years as coaches and parents, we find the preference for individual versus small group training to be split.

Many parents like the one-to-one attention of an individual training session. For players who need to work on basic ball mastery skills, this is your best option. The point of these sessions is not to get 3,000 touches in an hour. Rather, it's to identify technical errors, correct the flaws, and start to establish positive striking habits.

Players should always look to improve the quality of their touches, but much of that can be done on an individual basis. Plus, with fantastic resources online, such as Beast Mode Soccer, Online Soccer Academy, and Yael Averbuch (all on YouTube), intermediate and advanced players have all the resources they need. As long as the internal motivation is there, your son or daughter will not lack resources.

Small group training (four to 12 players) is our preferred option. For players with even the very basics of ball manipulation, these sessions allow for small-sided games. Within the games, players are given the context to perform their technical actions while improving their soccer IQ. Contextualizing development is the fastest means of improvement. As players complete the technical actions that fit the context of the game, you'll see your child completing more challenging passes while also processing the spatial and temporal challenges presented by an opponent.

Again, we're looking for a holistic approach to player development. Small group training, in addition to saving you some money, hits all four of the developmental pillars. It's the quickest path for player development and more closely models the game.

Available Resources online

To round out this section on personal training, We want to list the online resources in one place to help your child take charge of their development. We've already mentioned some resources, but will include them here just so you have each listing in one spot. All recommendations can be found on YouTube.

CaptainElite.com

SoccerRenegade.com

Beast Mode Soccer

Online Soccer Training

Yael Averbuch

Become Elite

Coerver Coaching

Total Football Analysis

Summary

1. Self-training is the easiest place to start, as well as a barometer for gauging their hunger for personal development.
2. Pickup and futsal are underutilized resources for soccer development, as are other sports. They're a great way to expedite improvement and have fun.
3. Personal training is another option if the desire and funds are there. Ideally, these training sessions will hit upon the four pillars of development. A great way to cut costs and get more out of these paid sessions is to prioritize small group sessions over individual.

Goalkeeper Training

The goalkeeper is the fireman of the team. They only get called into action when there are mistakes that need to be fixed. At best, they have 5-6 opportunities to make a huge difference during 90+ minutes of a game. The position is completely unique in that the technical skills, positioning, communication, and physical attributes are like no other on the pitch. The mentality is different as there is a tendency towards responsibility, leadership, and grit. The position usually picks the player rather than the player picks the position.

Sometimes, coaches approach outfield players to play keeper as they need someone to tend the goal. If your player has even a little interest, encourage them to try the position for a while. Make an agreement with the coach that the player will try the position for a few weeks and to meet again to decide what to do. During that time, learn more about the position by focusing on the keeper during matches in person or on TV. In the end, let the player decide, not anyone else. It should be a calling.

Many parents worry about how dangerous the position is. While there are the possibilities of catastrophic injuries, keepers tend to get injured less than outfield players based on our experience. It seems like there are fewer overuse injuries and collisions than other types of players. Keepers usually become durable and learn the important life skill of how to fall. Keepers tend to be more responsible and the position develops leadership skills. Based on Chris's experience, the players take roles of leadership such as senior execs or executive directors.

Let's imagine that your player really wants to play the position. Most parents are at a loss what to do.

Many clubs want to have great keepers but may not have the money to invest in them. Goalkeepers represent less than 9% of the player pool and require separate coaches, need field space, and additional equipment. Goalkeeper scheduling is difficult as team coaches want keepers for most of the training. As a result, goalkeeper training can have more than 8 keepers per coach at irregular hours only a couple of times weekly. This situation creates an opportunity...

Your player can get ahead if they have the passion and work ethic for the keeper position in ways other players cannot. The numerous technical elements of the position, such as how to catch the ball, stance, diving, high balls, and distribution, need lots of repetitions which will not be achieved in team practice. For this reason, a keeper should be doing specific training at least 3x weekly for under 13 years old and 4X weekly for above 13 years old.

Most likely, your player will have to find supplemental training. Some clubs offer additional keeper training, but, in all likelihood, you will have to find private goalkeeper training which will charge by the session. These weekly trainings are foundational for the steady development of your keeper. For example, two supplemental trainings on top of the regular two club trainings translate into your player getting 100% more training than peers. The benefits will be obvious after six months and remarkable over 3-4 years. Summer camps are great for the all-encompassing experience to get great instruction and realize that there are others that love the position. There are online resources where players (and their parents) can watch videos to understand the theory and drills.

Other types of training are also very helpful. Lateral (side-to-side) agility training can make a big difference, particularly during and post-puberty. Other sports, basketball and tennis, in particular, are great for cross-training and should be done as long as realistically possible.

The investment in goalkeeper and lateral agility training is the best return on time and money.

I find two areas that are under-coached in goalkeeping: confidence management and anticipation. These areas are covered elsewhere in the book. However, confidence management is so important for the "fireman" on the team. It is important to reiterate that perfection is the enemy of innovation. Encourage your player to take chances and try something new. Make many mistakes, but not the same ones again and again. Replay the game's events, learn from them, and then forget about the events. Encourage the players to adapt to the game rather than be stuck on having a clean sheet (no goals scored on them). Foster the mindset that they are there to win the game and not avoid losing. It will be liberating.

More than likely, your player will play on a weaker team where they get scored on often. This is a great opportunity. Keep in mind that your player's development is more valuable than who wins a game that no one will remember in three months. More reps are better for your keeper. Chris's son played on weaker teams for a couple of years. While it was tough at times, he gained tremendous confidence in chaotic situations where he had to step up. He developed resilience in preparation for when he moved to stronger teams. In fact, for academies in Germany's Bundesliga, they will take the stronger keepers and match them with the weaker teams.

The goalkeeper position offers a unique role to develop leadership skills as a difference-maker. Additional training will likely put your player at a tremendous advantage from a development perspective. Confidence management will be key.

Summary

1. If your child has an interest in playing goalkeeper, especially at a young age, encourage them to spend time in goal at practices and games, though preferably not full-time until they're in their teens.
2. Club-provided goalkeeper sessions should be prioritized. If your club doesn't offer goalie-specific training or if your child shows a strong desire for additional training, you can find goalkeeper coaches in your community to run supplemental sessions.
3. Athletic training and participation in other sports, especially basketball and tennis, can greatly benefit your young athlete.

Tactical Study

Tactical periodization is the tool coaches use to rotate their tactical topics at practices and ensure the team develops in a well-balanced manner. It's also a great tool our kids can use at home to develop their understanding of the game.

All your child has to do, and you can help them if they're in one of the younger age groups, is identify some level-appropriate ideas that they can study. And no, study does not mean the U12s need to open up a dense tactics book and take notes.

The easiest way to include tactical periodization through home training is to have your child write down some of the most important ideas their team is working on. If Coach Rodrigo has little Maddie's team working on building out of the back, have her write down some of the patterns that were often repeated and the coaching points that she heard.

Next, kick back, relax, and watch a soccer game with her. As she watches the game, have her focus on just that one aspect. As either of the two teams builds out of the back, ask what she's seeing. Better yet, if you live near a professional soccer team, take her to a game. The live experience is an eye-opener for kids.

As little Maddie becomes a teenager, especially if she's serious about progressing in the game, there are more tactics books than she can possibly read. Asking a coach or director for a recommendation, something like Revitalizing Real Madrid or subscribing to Total Football Analysis, is the best way to go. There's a lot of noise, so it's worth asking someone who's entrenched in the game to help you see through it to find the signal.

Watching the game is one of the best ways to improve tactical knowledge. That said, the way you watch the game is equally important. Don't get stuck on watching the ball. Going in looking for specific topic will help. Here's a list for your player's tactical study.

Individual Tactics/Soccer IQ

Beginner

Angles

Notice the short and intermediate range movements players make to create new angles for passes, shots, dribbles, tackles, interceptions, and blocking passing lanes.

Depth/Height

How deep (close to his goal) does Player X position himself in Y scenarios? How high (close to the opponent's goal)?

Improvisation

Analyze the various techniques and tricks players use to escape difficult situations.

Pinning

Restraining a defender from defending against two viable options, committing them to defending against one action (like a pass) in order to take another action (like a dribble). Pinning can also leave players in no-mans-land, undecided on which option to defend against, leaving them flat-footed.

Scanning

Scanning is a critical view of the field that allows a player to create a mental representation of the field. Short, intermediate, and long-distance playing opportunities are informed by scanning and processing information.

Width

How does Player X manage the width of the pitch within his role?

Intermediate

Action vs Passivity

Closely related to timing and spatial orientation, studying action vs passivity comes down to identifying when players are best suited to take action (checking to the ball, running into space, adapting positioning, etc.) as opposed to staying in place (let defense's movement create a gap, defender sticks with you which creates room for a teammate, opposing winger stays in wing but you're better off protecting the middle, etc.).

Balance

Study how a player's balance, or lack of it, determines their success in tackling, 1v1s, passing accuracy, and shooting. You will find that better physical balance correlates to greater success in actions.

Body Orientation

Watch how body orientation, the direction a player faces, impacts their personal speed of play. Action and directional efficiency, as well as quickness of action and release, are the keys.

Decision Making

What are the conditions that cue a winger to engage in a 1v1? What does a midfielder need to see before he directs the team to move forward? How does a defender gain half a second to intercept a pass? Ask who, what, when, where, why, and how when studying a specific player's decision making.

Mobility

How do contrasting levels of mobility impact the way two players operate in the same tactical role?

Timing

Syncing individual actions, such as passing and tackling, to coincide with optimal opportunities for action.

Advanced

4 Reference Points/Analyzing Play

Assess the tactical engagement of a player through their orientation to 1) the ball, 2) teammates, 3) the opponent, and 4) space. See image and full description on page 100.

Deception

Soccer is as mental a sport as you'll find. Watch how players use deception to win 1v1s and pull opponents away from the space they want to attack.

Dragging

Moving away from the space you or a teammate want to attack, pulling your mark with you. Examples include a winger pulling an outside-back into the wing or an attacking midfielder dragging the defensive midfielder high up the pitch.

Perception

Following from scanning, top players have the ability to scan the environment, identify key information, and filter out the rest. As players scan the pitch, can you identify which cues and patterns they're looking for?

Spatial Orientation

This is the way a player positions himself within the opposition's defensive shape. Optimal spatial orientation creates more time and space for that specific player or one of his teammates.

Tempo

The game is played at different speeds, ranging from end-to-end fast paced play to a slow tempo allowing players to catch their breath. It can also lull an opponent to sleep before a fast-paced attack. Which players set the tempo and how do they do it?

Team Tactics

Beginner

Building out of the Back

Connecting deep in a team's end of the field as they prepare to attack the opponent. What does the team's attacking shape look like and how successful are they in baiting the opposition forward? Can they effectively play out of the high press?

Counterattacking

A direct attack immediately after recovering the ball, striking before the opponent has a chance to organize. See full reference on page 84.

Counterpressing

Pressing the opposition's counterattack. See full reference on page 85.

Defending in Three Channels

Reference the "Field of Play" image on page 43. The field is split into five vertical channels (two wings, two half spaces, and the central channel) and a team should defend in three consecutive zones. For example, if the ball is in the middle of the pitch, the defending team should have all players in the central channel and two half spaces.

Height/Depth

A team's positioning at the top of the vertical axis. Study team structure or break it into lines, such as midfielders. How do teams manage their height along the vertical axis, both in attack and defense? As opposed to height, depth is the better end of the vertical axis. Here you'd want to study how teams keep their lines connected vertically, both in attack and defense.

Width

Width is the team's occupation of the horizontal axis. Most are wide in attack and narrow in defense. Studying width in transitions from attack to defense, and vice versa, is a great tactical study.

Intermediate

Attacking the Goal

Encompasses the final pass, but includes the entire sequence of movements leading to an attack on goal. Follows from the "attacking the opponents" phase of play.

Connecting the Lines

Link up play, especially from the midfielders and outside-backs, to help the possessing team progress up field. Study how teams connect the lines as they attack the opponent.

Possession to Penetrate

Using possession as a tool for disorganizing the opposition, then transitioning into a direct attack once they've lost their defensive shape.

Press: High/Medium/Low

The third of the pitch where teams engage defensively. See full reference on page 55.

Pressure/Cover/Balance

Pressure on the ball, coverage for the pressure defender, and the support system. How do teams use these principles to secure themselves defensively? See full reference on page 51.

The Final Ball/Pass

The coordinated runs and pass that lead to a goal-scoring

opportunity. See full reference on page 45.

Advanced

4 Superiorities

Numeric, positional, qualitative, and socio-affective advantages. See full reference on page 102.

Defensive Funneling

Guiding the opposition's attack into a preferred area for pressuring the ball. Some teams like to force opponents into the wings before applying pressure on the ball carrier, some want the opponent to play into the center so that three midfielders can work towards a recovery.

Overload to Unbalance

Overloading is the act of committing numbers to a specific area of the field. Overload to unbalance refers to creating a numeric superiority near the ball in order to draw the opposition's defense forward. As they commit too many players to the ball, their defensive shape lacks structure, or balance, as they are overcommitted in a specific area. Once opponents are unbalanced, the possessing team is cued to play forward through the unbalanced (remember pressure/cover/balance?) lines of the opposition. See full reference on page 55.

Positional Rotations and Interactions

Players swapping roles, such as a left-back moving into the left-forward's space, the box-to-box midfielder (#8) dropping deeper to cover the space the left-back vacated, and the left-forward moving centrally into the #8's space to free up the wing for the left-back. Closely linked positions will interact throughout the game, moving off of each other and creating space for a teammate's benefit.

Spatial Occupation

How a team fills the pitch, such as a central overload with one width provider on each wing. Each phase of attack and defense brings about specific spatial occupation demands.

Tempo

The pace, or speed, at which the game is played. Look for playing styles and objectives in high, medium, and low tempo teams. Additionally, can you identify cues that signal a team to change the tempo, such as a low tempo build-out to a high tempo direct attack?

Finding the right player and team to study is a big part of the process too. If you're not comfortable making a player comparison, have your child ask their coach for one. If Seth is a Christian Pulisic Mini-Me, encourage him to watch Pulisic's games, identifying what works with that skill set and what doesn't.

That's the player side of the process. You then want to find a team that's similar in style to your child's team. One important note here is to idealize with the team choice. My kid's team might not look like Real Madrid, but if the coach wants them to play that way and models his playing style after that club, kids need to see what the end product looks like. Quite frankly, parents and coaches can benefit from that as well. Just like the kids, it's good to look at what works and what doesn't within a specific style of play.

> **Watch players who are at your level and look at their decisions, then talk about it and watch the NWSL or the Premier League players that are in your positions. What makes them so good? What do you think their tactical goals were at the beginning of the game? What did they execute well? I think having conversations about soccer and about games that you've watched can be really educational. And while yes, I think you need to have a knack for it at times, you can definitely learn those skills of recognizing the opponent and recognizing what's on.**
>
> **-Sam Mewis**

Studying the tactical side of the game is often overlooked at the youth level, especially here in the USA. But we're telling you, kids with high soccer IQs and an understanding of complex tactics really shine, sometimes even more so than kids who are exceptional athletes or highly technical players. Knowing the ins and outs of the game, especially how it applies to your child's role on the field is a massive differentiator.

Summary

1. Smarter players have a massive advantage over their peers. Playing is the quickest way to make progress, but watching the game, focusing on one tactical idea at a time, can greatly enhance their understanding of the game.
2. Make it fun by watching your favorite teams and players together, especially if their playing philosophy is similar to what your child's team is trying to achieve.
3. Idealize when you watch the games. Having the end in mind gives clear indications of how to bridge the gap between your child's present and endpoint.

SECTION FOUR:
Wrapping Up

College Pathways

Most kids dream and many parents hope that college and pro soccer are possible. In reality, over 95% of youth athletes will not play college ball. Fewer than 2% will play professionally. The numbers are sobering.

Most families think of college soccer as only Division 1; however, there are Division 2, Division 3, NAIA, and NJCAA (junior college).

The truth is that your player may be able to play college ball if your family is open to playing for colleges at different levels.

As far as college scholarships, the probabilities are much higher that your player will get more scholarship money from putting the extra effort into better grades and testing. Division 1 women's and men's soccer programs can have up to 14 and 9.9 scholarships, respectively. Soccer programs are a cost center for universities as nearly all programs lose money. College football, basketball, and some baseball programs pay the bills for all the other sports. Most soccer programs are underfunded with high turnover of assistant coaches because of low or no pay.

For these reasons, head coaches are overworked managing what happens on the pitch and making ends meet off it. Summer camps are important for coaches' income to make it all work. Assistant coaches work really hard for a little recognition and even less money. Assistant coaches are responsible for setting up training sessions, managing players, operations, and recruiting. These coaches are the front line for recruiting where programs will get 100 emails daily from prospective recruits. Like other enterprises, the coaches have to recruit and retain the best talent they can find, afford, and who have good enough grades.

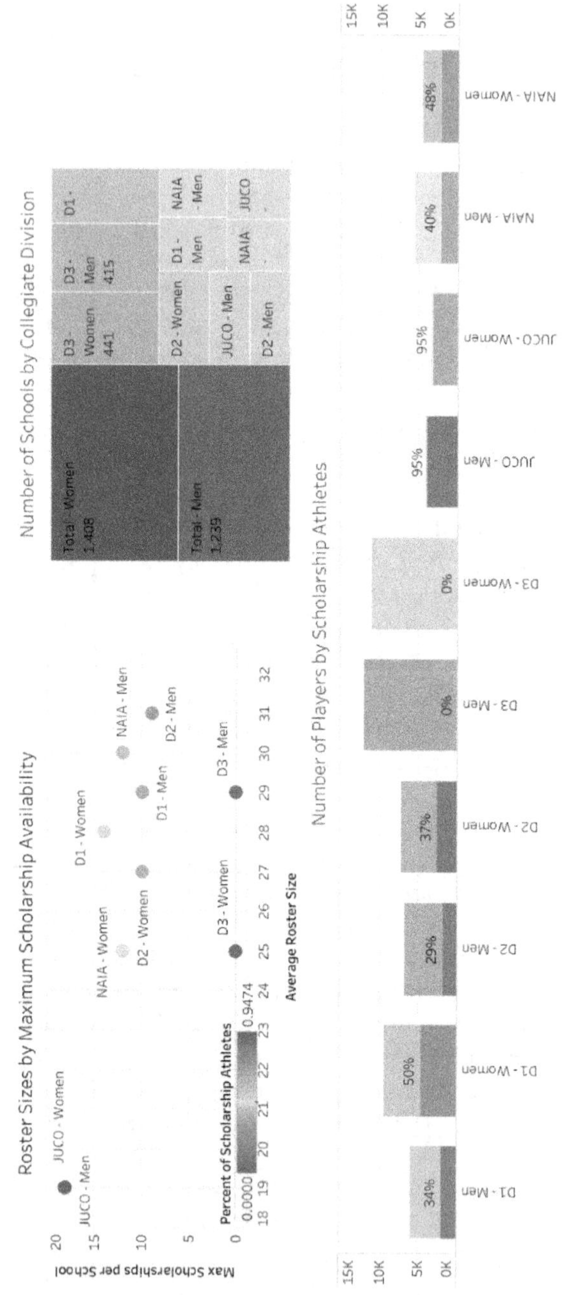

Number of Schools by Collegiate Division
Total - Women 1,408
Total - Men 1,239
D3 - Women 441
D3 - Men 415
D2 - Women
D1 - Women
D1 - Men
D2 - Men
JUCO - Men
NAIA - Men
NAIA
JUCO
Roster Sizes by Maximum Scholarship Availability
Max Scholarships per School
20
15
10
5
0
JUCO - Women
JUCO - Men
D1 - Women
NAIA - Women
D2 - Women
NAIA - Men
D1 - Men
D2 - Men
D3 - Women
D3 - Men
Average Roster Size
18 19 20 21 22 23 24 25 26 27 28 29 30 31 32
Percent of Scholarship Athletes
0.0000 0.9474
Number of Players by Scholarship Athletes
15K
10K
5K
0K
D1 - Men 34%
D1 - Women 50%
D2 - Men 29%
D2 - Women 37%
D3 - Men 0%
D3 - Women 0%
JUCO - Men 95%
JUCO - Women 95%
NAIA - Men 40%
NAIA - Women 48%

Each year, colleges will have somewhat different priorities in terms of players. This year, they may be looking for a striker or centerback. Next year, it may be midfielders. The matchup may often not work for the college and year your player wants to attend.

College showcases are the primary way for coaches to recruit players. Think of these events as huge job marketplaces. There is a hierarchy of these tournaments: MLS, Generation Adidas, ECNL, Dallas Cup, and Jefferson Cup, to name a few. These events are efficient in that coaches can see many players in person all on several trips.

National team players

College coaches are well aware of national team players by following national team rosters and national team player pools. These players are recruited by MLS academies and top college programs

MLS Academies

College coaches go to these Academy Showcases. The MLS Academies hold on to their best players - likely fewer than 10% - by offering pro contracts and encouraging the rest to play college ball for their development. Top college programs are dialed into these players starting at U16 and aggressively in at U17 while finding last-minute pick-ups at U19.

ECNL, USL, and Regional Tournaments

College coaches at all levels attend these tournaments. Each has their own network of youth coaches to help identify players.

Based on conversations with college coaches, recruitment is usually 75% from seeing players at tournaments, 15% that attend college ID camps, and 10% random, including recommendations of youth coaches.

Start the college consideration process in earnest during sophomore year of high school. Puberty will have a huge impact on the prospects. Visit colleges and attend games so your player has a clearer understanding of what college is and the levels required.

COLLEGE RECRUITMENT TIMELINE

BEFORE STARTING SOPHOMORE YEAR
- Pursue Healthy Lifestyle
- Academic Achievement
- Fall in Love with the Game
- Commit to Extra Training
- Explore Interest in the College Game

FALL SOPHOMORE YEAR
- Pursue Healthy Lifestyle
- Academic Achievement
- Determine 20 School Universe

SPRING SOPHOMORE YEAR
- Pursue Healthy Lifestyle
- Academic Achievement
- Collect Video
- Register for Summer ID Camps

FALL JUNIOR YEAR
- Pursue Healthy Lifestyle
- Academic Achievement
- Introductory Emails
- Follow-Up Emails
- Texts (Coach led)
- Calls (Coach led)
- Unofficial Visits

SPRING JUNIOR YEAR
- Pursue Healthy Lifestyle
- Academic Achievement
- Introductory Emails
- Follow-Up Emails
- Texts (Coach led)
- Calls (Coach led)
- Official and Unofficial Visits
- Register for Summer ID Camps

FALL SENIOR YEAR
- Pursue Healthy Lifestyle
- Academic Achievement
- Official and Unofficial Visits
- Signing Period

SPRING SENIOR YEAR
- Pursue Healthy Lifestyle
- Academic Achievement
- Signing Period
- Increase Training Intensity
- Get into the Best Shape of Your Life, Then Add Another 30%

Here is how the process generally works: college coaches only start to focus on students during the fall of their junior year on the boys' side, sophomore year for the girls. The prime recruitment time is during the spring of junior year and fall of senior year. As a result, tournaments and college ID camps take center stage. The traditional recruitment model was for players to wait for college coaches to discover and contact them. In our opinion, that model is as relevant as a belle waiting for someone to ask them to the ball. Unless you are a national team player or high-level NWSL/MLS academy player, then your player will have to join the 21st Century and build awareness of their playing to coaches.

Here is a checklist of things to do for college ball.

Reality Check

This is one of the most difficult things to evaluate. How does your player compare to other college-bound players? Here is how to research:

1. Look up the rosters of colleges that your player wants to attend. Write down the clubs and levels of the current players, particularly the one that plays your player's position. Are they mostly NWSL or MSL academy players, ECNL, or other levels?
2. Find out what colleges your club's players have attended in past years. Is your player on the same trajectory in terms of the club's first or second team?
3. Attend college matches to get a sense of the speed, technical skills, and positioning. How does your player compare?
4. Talk to your player's coach about your player's prospects. Keep in mind they may be polite. Ask for the unvarnished truth on what level is possible.

Everybody has a different perspective. It's a nervous time and it's difficult. You have to understand communication is crucial, so is understanding where you are and being realistic. One of the things I ask all my kids that come to camp is to look carefully at the

individuals playing the game and understand, "do you really see yourself out there? Are you good enough to play at this level?"

Try to get to as many games as you can so that you can really decipher if you're at that level or not. And then the next thing you have to decipher is "are you just barely good enough or are you better than what's out there?"

A lot of kids kind of kid themselves on thinking that "I can play here," but the reality is they probably can't. Understand that the coach is looking for the next best player, not the same level. I already have enough of these players on my team, now I'm looking for better players. So it's a challenge to gather all this information, digest it, and come to a reality.

It's a process, and certainly lean on folks that you know that have been through the process and can help you gauge reality. Don't be afraid to ask questions. A lot of parents are still wondering what's going on and sometimes they might not like the answer to their questions, but you have to be prepared for that as well. It's not an easy process. I find it difficult even from my side when I'm in control of the process. It's unnerving at times and I feel for a lot of the parents. It's a big decision and, in many cases, a decision that's going to cost a lot of money. It's a very challenging time, so try to educate yourself as much as you can and ask questions. Be ready for whatever answer is told and move forward.

-John Kerr
Duke University Men's Soccer Coach and Former US Men's National Team Player

National Team Pool or NWSL/MLS academies

Your player will have strong prospects for a D1 college program if they have good grades.

ECNL

Your player could have decent prospects for D1 and strong prospects for D2 and D3 if they play for a strong club and are one of the best players on the team.

Elite/Premier

Your player could play for D2 and D3 colleges if your child plays for a strong club and is one of the best players on the team.

A good target is for your player to be on the first U17 ECNL team of your club to play college soccer.

You've probably noticed that high school soccer didn't make the list. Kerr mentioned that he rarely recruits high school-only players, which is a common trend at the top of the collegiate game, noting, "Most kids know that if you want to play at the top levels of college soccer, you have to be doing more than just high school soccer." If your athlete is a high school only player, ID camps and reaching out to coaches is incredibly important. Even still, know that the upper echelons of the college game are likely out of reach.

20 School Universe

Based on your realistic assessment, you can create a range of schools which include stretch schools, core targets, and fallbacks. Consider the size of the school, location, professor-to-student ratio, reputation, relevant majors, and cost. Your player likely has 3-4 schools in mind. Expand the options by considering other colleges that are in the same conference as your player's favorite schools. In the end, the best school is the one that wants your player and your player wants it back. They have to want the position that year while your player has to want the program. Be sure to research the team rosters to understand what year the players are and their previous soccer clubs.

> **One of the things I always ask folks is, "what do they want out of their experience?" Different people will give you different answers because some kid's goals aren't to start at their college right away in their freshman year. Others are happy enough to try to get to that school of their choice and fight for a spot and get more playing time as they go.**
>
> **-John Kerr**

Collect videos

During Sophomore spring semester, collect video of your player. Many clubs often capture video of high-level games. You could spend lots of money on video equipment. A quick and easy solution is to buy a GoPro camera, or low-cost equivalent, and an inexpensive tripod. Be sure to practice recording while experimenting with the location and lighting. Don't aim the camera into the light. Be sure to capture the full range of your player. Just make sure your camera is designed for high-pace action.

Encourage your player to learn how to edit video. Good recruit videos can be done with apps such as iMovie or WeVideo.

The video should be no longer than 3 minutes. In the intro, add a title with your player's name, club, date, and contact info. The main segments should include the highlights. In the outro, include your player's grades and contact info. Have your player create a few of these videos to work out the kinks before showing to college coaches. Get feedback from their current club coaches.

> **The process itself started a lot earlier for my daughter than my son. That's still probably the case today with college recruiters looking at girls that are in eighth, ninth, and 10th grade. On the boys' side, I don't really look too closely until the spring of their 10th-grade year.**
>
> **Candidly, it's because there's such a change in the physical development of boys in that age bracket. So, my daughter's recruiting process ended up being a lot**

earlier and, therefore, we did a lot more ID camps for exposure.

-John Kerr

Emails

Starting in September of your player's junior year, send an introductory email to the head coach and recruiting coach. Here are the recommended contents:

<u>First Email</u>

Title: Player name, position, and the first year that you plan to start college

Intro paragraph: Write a short (no more than six lines) introduction of your soccer experience, course names, and your GPA. Include any shared connections (like a coach) if you have any. When possible, add key tournament dates and video links.

Contact information: Include player's phone number and coach's email and cell number

Video: No more than 3 minutes of highlights in different phases: passing, shooting, defending.

<u>Follow up Emails</u>

Frequency: Sent out monthly if you have video highlights

Title: Player name, position, and college start year

Update paragraph: Write a short (no more than six lines) update which includes recent tournaments you have attended and updated GPA.

Video: No more than three minutes of highlights in different phases

These emails are key to build awareness of your player. The goal is for your player to be top of mind when a need for the position arises. Starting at the end of fall junior year, request a transcript from your school. Your player should register for the NCAA during spring of their junior year.

Texts

If a coach is interested, they will likely text or call you to get to know the player. Often, a coach will set up a call and then check in via texts. Keep all communications professional.

Calls

Regular calls from the coach are a sign of significant interest. Keep the communications personable and professional.

General types of questions that coaches ask:

What motivates you to play?
What kind of teammate are you?
How do you handle pressure?
What is a recent setback and how did you overcome it?
What type of training do you do?
What are your likes and dislikes?

Players should practice answering these questions several times with parents, mentors, or coaches.

Questions that you could ask a coach:

First conversation
What is the style of play?
What do you look for in a player (in your position like defender, midfielder, forward, etc)?
What is the depth in the current position?

Follow up conversations
How do current players manage the school vs soccer balance?
What academic support is there for soccer players?

Be prepared for these texts and calls to be on and off. Coaches are busy and likely talking to other recruits as well.

College Visits

According to the NCAA, there are two types of visits: official and unofficial. An official visit is when the college pays expenses for a prospective student-athlete to visit. These include transportation, lodging, meals, and entertainment (including three tickets to a home game). Parent expenses are not covered. Prospective student-athletes are allowed to take a maximum of five official visits to five different schools (only one official visit per school). Official visits usually happen in junior and senior years.

Unofficial visits are those where the prospective student-athlete's family bears the cost of the visit. An unlimited number of unofficial visits are possible.

During visits, prospective student-athletes often stay with one current student who is on the team. Sometimes, multiple students will show you around so you get a feel for the players. Activities include a tour of the university, meeting with coaches and professors, watching a practice or game, attending class, and getting a taste of the social scene. These visits can last a few hours but no more than 48 hours. These visits are important to help determine the fit between the prospective student-athlete, coaches, current players, and school.

Offers

There are two types of offers: a verbal offering, which is non-binding, and National Letter of Intent (NLI), which is a legally binding agreement between the college and athlete. Not all D1/D2 colleges use NLI so check with the institution.

The signing period is November 11 - August 1 of the senior academic year and summer of the player.
There are different types of offers to play in college:

Full Scholarship

D1 programs can offer up to 14 scholarships for women's and 9.9 for men's soccer.
D2 programs can offer up to 9 scholarships for women's and men's soccer.
D3 does not offer scholarships.

Full scholarships are rare. Expenses covered include tuition, room and board, books, and fees. These are one-year contracts renewed annually.

Partial Scholarship

Programs often spread the money around the team to help more players. In August 2020, regulations changed so student-athletes needs and academic scholarships could be supplemented with athletic scholarships. Previously, all scholarships would be counted against the soccer program's scholarships.

Recruited Walk-On

Programs can offer a player a roster spot with no financial assistance. If a player does well, then a scholarship could be offered.

Unrecruited Walk-On

A program may invite a player to try out for a roster spot in the preseason. Coaches will often confirm a tryout invite prior to enrollment.

The recruiting process is full of starts and stops. Be proactive, positive, and patient. Your player's goal is to make the recruitment process as easy as it can be for coaches. Their situations can be fluid - coaching changes, current college players leaving school, and new recruits becoming available. You are trying to help the coaches solve their recruiting problem.

Over time, your player should work hard to find matches for several schools. Once the offers become real, then consider the following.

1. How is the college learning environment?
2. Does the campus fit your preference of where you want to go to college?
3. What programs are appealing?
4. How important is playing time in the first couple of years?
5. How do you compare to current players in your position?
6. What is the energy of the team?
7. What is the feel that you get from the coaches?
8. How do you feel about the practice facilities and game field?

It's always worrisome when players and families get their hearts set on one college. A player often determines their top choice school based on their parent's alma maters or the college's football or basketball team.

As far as scholarships, your player may be better served putting the time into academic financial aid based on grades and test scores. Needs-based financial aid can go a long way. Don't allow your player to get caught up on the status of being a scholarship or full scholarship athlete.

The perfect school is one where the coaches want you and the player wants to be at the school. It is much more important to find the right fit between the player, coaches, other players, playing time prospects, and finances.

Realize that in today's world, college sports may not necessarily be what it was like when the parents played. It is almost a full-time job. There are expectations that the players are committed to helping their teammates win on the field of play. So, from that perspective, it's not a deterrent, but it's an acknowledgment that you're going to be focused, you're expected to contribute, and you're going to get some huge benefits from it.

-Skip Gilbert

Summary

1. Go into the recruitment process with a clear plan. Outline deadlines, schedule game recordings, prepare your profile, and create your 20 School Universe. And don't forget to prioritize academics as those scholarships are far more valuable than athletic scholarships.
2. Prioritize your communication with the coaches. Send updates and try to visit the campus through official and unofficial visits. Your child should have clear answers to the questions in this chapter and follow the communication guidelines.
3. Finding the right fit has to be the top priority. Chasing more prestigious schools is pointless if the fit isn't right. Your child will be happiest and most productive in an environment that fits their academic and athletic needs.

Mental Health

As we approach the end of the book, we're going to finish with the two most important topics, the mental health of our children and reframing our view of sports in order to establish a deeper relationship with them so that we can guide them to become the best versions of themselves.

As technology advances and information becomes more accessible and spreads more quickly, we are seeing an epidemic of mental health across the globe. Adolescent depression and anxiety are skyrocketing and suicide rates are climbing, even among our preteens, a demographic that has joined this worrisome conversation for the first time in human history.

Though the causes of childhood depression and anxiety extend well beyond sports, we want to 1) ensure that our approach to sports and sports parenting isn't contributing to the problem and, 2) rather than taking a negative view and saying, "how can we make sure youth sports doesn't overwhelm our kids," there's an opportunity for us to flip the script and ask, "how can youth sports help my child develop into a virtuous human being?"

Starting with the end in mind, there's an opportunity for us to see how youth sports participation contributes to the development of our children. We shouldn't settle for any less. The stakes are simply too high.

As you read through this chapter, there is a need to detach from visions of grandeur. Only a small percentage of players will reach the pros or the collegiate level, so that can't be the primary purpose of youth sport participation. It's inherently exclusive as only the top players reach those levels. However, if we reframe our view of youth sports to help our kids become the best version of themselves that they can possibly be and learn how to maintain their mental health along the way, that's an objective that everyone can reach, and it all starts with the internal narrative.

The Internal Narrative

> I have a specific memory of playing in a State Cup in Oregon. We were playing against a team called Corvallis, which was the other good team in the state. I don't know if it was the semifinals or the finals, but I just remember that I was well aware I was the best player on the field.
>
> All I could hear for the entire game is screaming parents, telling their kids to force me to my right foot and screaming that I was getting advantages. I remember it being a really bizarre experience for a 10 or 11-year-old to have an entire bench and team literally targeting me for an entire game for the sake of winning…and parents screaming, like the entire bench of the other team, screaming at me.
>
> The fact that I remember it is what I think is the problem. I've had a lot of incredible memories as a soccer player and in my life, but the fact that things like that stand out is kind of traumatic. They're kind of traumatic when I look back at them and think, "I wasn't going to have to beat the other team for us to win. I was going to have to beat them, beat the parents, beat the other coach, beat the ref..." And you know, when you're competing, it's just a lot to take on. I could feel attacks happening the whole game.
>
> -Heath Pearce

Heath, who's work at For Soccer Ventures seeks to drive participation and fanbase growth of the American game, was an elite youth player, so he had to deal with a little more verbal abuse than most of us. Unfortunately, his story is a common one across the youth sports landscape. Not only are kids experiencing this disturbing level of disrespect and abuse as a direct result of their participation in youth sports, but these children who are still largely unskilled in the mental side of the game have to combat these thoughts psychologically.

And we're not just talking about our high school level athletes. Even our entry-level children experience this level of hostility. If you're at a U6 through U10 rec game, just take a moment to listen to the sidelines. While our kids don't pick up everything that is said, they'll hear enough, which alters the way they look at themselves and their interactions within the game.

The internal narrative is the running dialogue a person has with themselves. As Heather Waters notes, "at some point the game turns from physical ability to mental toughness," making a healthy internal narrative central to your child's success. Whether at work, school, or on the soccer pitch, we're always formulating thoughts and interpreting the conditions of our environment. Ultimately, we want to know how we fit into the bigger picture.

At times, our thoughts become so focused on the bigger picture, that we lose sight of things that are within our control. We may have some say in the bigger picture, but, ultimately, we won't have much control of the many moving parts within the greater ecological dynamics. From an internal narrative standpoint, we can become overwhelmed with our lack of control over the situation and become distracted in our mission, to own our thoughts and actions while controlling how we engage the people, environments, and situations we encounter.

Alternative Interactions

> **There are a lot of parents who get caught up with "Are you starting today? What's the position that you're playing today? Why aren't you starting today?" That creeps into a player's psyche as they go into games, "Hey, I loved watching you play today and thought you gave great effort. I'm really proud of you. Let's go get a hot dog," or whatever he wants to do. It becomes this tension of always, I got to answer for something from the player's perspective, and that's an area I think we can all be better at.**
>
> **-Gary Buete**

This quote from Gary serves to reinforce the point we've made throughout the book, which is to let the player relax and process the game on the drive home and take a player-led approach to discussing the match. The underlying point is that many players view the car ride as an interrogation. They don't want to be there and they certainly don't want to answer performance-related questions, be it about team or individual.

Scott fondly remembers listening to Oakland A's games with his Dad as they drove to and from games. Although Scott enjoyed a quick recap of the game and asking situation-specific questions of his former semi-pro playing Dad, it's those conversations about their favorite baseball team that dominated many car rides.

When they weren't talking about the A's, they might talk about Scott's social interests, debate the golden era of country music, their faith, or any of the other sports they both followed. The options are endless, but going in with a plan is a priority. The better you do in creating that bond, the easier it is to have the inevitable difficult conversations with your kids.

On the drive there, carpooling with the kid's friends is a great way to relieve the tension and limit game-specific talking. If you're traveling alone or as a family, music, podcasts, a game, and quiet time for preparation are often the best alternatives.

Guiding Your Athlete

In college, I was the person that was so laser-focused, even obsessed with winning. And it wasn't about winning at the time. I wanted to win a national championship. I wanted to be the best at Notre Dame. I wanted to win, win, win.

I wish I could go back and just shift my mentality a little bit. I wouldn't change anything, because I am who I am today and I'm proud of that, but I wish I could just shift it a little bit so that I wasn't so obsessed with soccer and, even on days where soccer wasn't going well, I could leave the field and still find ways to fulfill myself as a human being. I think I would punish myself, either if I didn't play well or if my team didn't win. I wouldn't go hang with my friends or go get ice cream or do whatever. And it's like, "Why? Why don't you just go enjoy your life? You're going to be young once and if something fulfills you in a different way than sports, you might as well take advantage of it because that's only going to help you on the field."

2018 was my first year here with the North Carolina Courage and I was happy, but I wasn't as fulfilled and I didn't play as well. In 2019, I had all these other friends I was involved with in the community. I had friends away from the soccer team, did all these other cool things here, and played much better soccer. I just felt more light and free and had all these other outlets to let my mind go. So if I was really disappointed in a performance, in a funk, or felt like I was having self-doubts on the field, I could just get away and go play cards or hang out in the pool and just hit the reset button.

-Cari Roccaro
North Carolina Courage Midfielder and Soccer Resilience Ambassador

As Americans, we tend to hold a relentless work ethic. You probably know someone who brags about working 12-15 hour days, remember someone from college who was wholly consumed by achieving an overall 4.0, or an athlete whose obsession to reach the next level takes over their lives.

That player's drive, dedication, and determination are laudable, but up to a point. For the internally motivated child, one issue we've come across is the inability to disconnect from the obsession. The prize is always on the mind, as are the configurations of the path to attainment.

The positives are that these players know what they want, how to get there, and are willing to put in the necessary time and energy to make that happen.

The negative is that the relationships suffer and other important areas of life are pushed to the wayside. Then, as the goal is achieved or abandoned, marking the end of the project in either instance, there's nothing left to fall back on. As we see in Cari's case, even in the midst of the pursuit, setbacks and spells of underperformance are going to happen. Without relationships to fall back on, the downward spiral often continues until the player hits rock bottom. Having strong relationships and outlets outside of the game are incredibly important. An added bonus is the increase of focus and enjoyment of play when the player hits the field again.

If your child tends to sit at the other end of the spectrum, it might be time to sit down and discuss whether they still enjoy the game. If not, that's fine, but the search for the next extracurricular should more closely align with their passion. There should be something they want to work towards, to improve upon. Sports typically fill that competitive experience, but there are plenty of other outlets off the field and court.

Habits to Help the Kids Control Their Narrative

Language, presence of mind, and processing emotions are three keys to controlling the personal narrative. Much like technique and tactical understanding, these are mental skills that kids can and should train.

In terms of language, self-talk is our internal dialog. As a player whiffs on a pass, they might think, "Geez, I'm awful." That's an example of negative self-talk. A positive, growth-oriented response goes straight to what went wrong, "I lunged forward when making contact which turned my foot inward and caused me to send a weak pass wide of my target. I'll focus on my approach the next time I send a pass." Negative language is focused on the outcome, which is unchangeable. Positive language is forgiving while looking to correct course and not make the same mistake again.

Presence of mind is what allows kids to identify when they're moving into negative self-talk or seeing a spiral in performance. As emotions start to boil, people with a high degree of mental skill can see the pending pitfall and correct course.

But those emotions still require processing. Each person should experiment to find what works best for them. It could be prayer or meditation, possibly talking to a friend or family member.

For Cari, journaling was her preferred way to process her thoughts and emotions: "It doesn't always have to be a time where you're struggling on the field or having a bad day. You can write about the good memories too so you can hold on to those and remember them as well." At times, your child can write their way through a problem, but other times they may want to journal about how awesome their life is. Writing about the positives and negatives also prevents us from pigeon-holing the journal as a source for anger and frustration.

I did this random little study when COVID started. I interviewed 10 of my professional soccer-playing friends. Some of them were on my team here, some of them playing the MLS, some play for the women's national team. I asked them all if how they're doing on the field affects them off the field each day. And then I asked them what they do each day to make sure that it doesn't put them in a downward spiral where they can't perform. Basically, the theme was hitting the reset button and finding a way to do that and to have things that you're very passionate about outside of your sport so you don't feel like your self-worth and identity are tied to how you perform as an athlete.

When I was typing up the answers, I thought, "we all said the same thing in a different way. We all came to the same conclusion that you cannot feel your worth and value are tied to how you perform as an athlete, the accolades you get, or how many times you win." You have to find other things to do.

You must, must, must have at least two to three go-to things that will 99.9% make you smile if you're having a terrible day on the field. So no matter what I'm going

through on the field, even if I can't catch a break, I'm like, "well, it's Monday, The Bachelor's on tonight and I'm super excited." No matter what, I'm pumped to watch The Bachelor, even if I had the worst day ever.

So I think for anyone to have two to three things, maybe you call your best friend or maybe you go get an ice cream or whatever it is you need, have something like a coping mechanism, just something to make you smile to remind yourself it's going to be alright. I am who I am as a human being, as a daughter, a friend, a cousin…whatever I am, it's not defined by if I pass the ball well today on the field.

-Cari Roccaro

Summary

1. Helping our kids control their personal narrative can help them shut out the negative voices and stay focused on what they can control.
2. As parents, finding conversation topics outside of the player's or team's performance can build stronger relationships and lasting memories. It'll also give you a stronger voice when difficult conversations are needed.
3. Encourage your kid to try different methods for processing emotions. We don't want explosive habits to develop due to neglect, but we also don't want the emotions to control actions or kids to develop a sense of hopelessness. Finding an outlet to process emotions and thoughts is key.

A Realistic Plan to be Best Version of Self

Not everyone gets that much-desired college athletic scholarship. If you recall the demographics chart in the College Pathway chapter, you'll recall that very few make it to that level. Even fewer make it to the pros.

Knowing that most youth athletes will play their last competitive soccer game when they finish youth or high school soccer, reaching college or the pros can't be the primary objective. It inherently excludes the vast majority of youth athletes, so there has to be something bigger at the end of the tunnel.

Instead, the primary purpose of sports is developing virtue, sportsmanship, competitiveness, integrity, and prioritizing their physical and mental well-being. It's a tool for helping us become the best version of ourselves. If one kid is particularly gifted and progresses to the professional ranks, fantastic. He's the exception.

That doesn't make the millions of others failures. In this instance, failure would be engaging in the sport and not taking away lessons that are applicable elsewhere. All good things must come to an end, like competitive soccer, but the values and memories shouldn't.

Can we, as parents, help the game become a transformative experience for our kids? We think so. It's easier said than done, but here are some ideas.

There are so few players that make it into the college game. In our club alone, we've got about 13,000 players. Take this year, in a COVID-19 year, we have roughly 70 players who are going on to play in college. It's a big number for youth soccer clubs, but in the whole scheme of the number of players who participate or have participated at their age that have gotten to this level, it's so small. It's so small that it shouldn't be the priority at the end of the day.

-Gary Buete

Reframing Purpose in Youth Soccer

We want our kids to walk away from their soccer experience with a sense of pride in their accomplishments and see how their participation impacted them as a person. If you share these goals, knowing how the youth soccer experience fits into the bigger picture is the first step.

By reframing the purpose of youth soccer, seeing it as a means to an end, helping our children become the best version of themselves, it's easier to handle the inevitable setbacks and disappointments. In fact, like joy and fulfillment, we'll see hardships and struggles as opportunities for development rather than catastrophes. Rather than jumping to our kid's rescue any time they face hardship, we're giving them an opportunity to experience resistance in a controlled environment with low stakes. That's such a gift.

> As someone who kind of coasted through, was always good at soccer, committed to Notre Dame, played on all the youth national teams...I had a fairly good life, but I've also hit some adversity and I think those are the moments that I've grown the most and figured out who I really am.
>
> When you're in middle school and high school, adversity might look something like "oh, I don't understand my math homework. I need help with that." It's kind of a minuscule problem. That's still valid, but you're going to hit some adversity as you get older and those are the times where you're going to question yourself and your self-worth.
>
> But those are going to be the times where you grow the most and figure out what you're made of and who you are. Adversity is inevitable. It comes in many ways, shapes, and sizes, and might hit you right in the face.

> **But when it does, never stopped believing in yourself, because that's when you do grow the most. You'll look back at those times and say, "I'm glad that happened because look at me now."**
>
> **-Cari Roccaro**

Playing the Long-Game

We can't tell you how many parent-led discussions we've had about whether or not a player should quit the sport, even at a relatively young age, because they've "plateaued" developmentally. Parents often ask if playing the game is worth the commitment.

While we can't make a blanket statement for each situation, we do believe there's a teaching moment here. Life's travels will take us to many places, delivering a host of relationships and experiences. There will come times when relationships, careers, and interests plateau or we become stuck under the weight of a burden. Life will present us with all sorts of problems to solve and glass-ceilings limiting our progress.

Sports participation does the same thing. But, again, within the controlled, low-stakes environment of youth sports, our kids get a dose of the short-term conflicts. If we can help them look at those problems as part of the journey, we're helping them see that we can work through the issues life throws our way. As Cari says, "Relax, take a breath, figure it out. It's about the journey and the process versus just being perfect in the moment." Soccer, like life, can get messy, but developing the problem-solving skills and resilience to handle these issues can carry them through life's darkest days.

In the words of Sir Winston Churchill, "success is not final, failure is not fatal: it is the courage to continue that counts."

Let Them Experience Childhood

American youth soccer is a largely professionalized sphere. Clubs are big business, coaches make careers out of it, and there's a clear supply and demand factor. Even though club soccer is a highly structured business, it's important that we don't get caught in the hustle and bustle of club life. When youth soccer becomes the top priority, family life suffers and childhoods are lost.

We've already spoken about the physical and psychological benefits of playing multiple sports, but Sam Mewis, a World Cup winner, put it best, saying, "Getting to play basketball was so much fun and it almost was less pressure because I wasn't this national basketball standout. I just got to play and try to make layups and it just let me be a kid a little bit longer."

This goes for other sports and extracurriculars, such as the arts, friendships, and passion projects. They'll only be young once. Helping them experience work (soccer)/life balance as a kid will help them prioritize a healthy lifestyle as an adult.

Owning the Single-Sport Decision

When your child makes the jump to a single sport or activity, be it soccer or something else, let your kid have the final say in that decision and make them own it. As kids turn their focus to a single sport, there's a mental shift in the approach.

While it may have been just a fun activity in the past, making it the single sport tends to signal they want to take it more seriously. Keep in mind that their peers have a similar mindset. When our kids make the jump, the commitment to presence, contribution, and work rate is implied. They owe it to themselves and their teammates to engage at the highest level possible.

Parent/Child Relationship, Not Sports Parent/Athlete Relationship

Make the parent/child relationship the priority, not the sports parent/athlete relationship. Even when the challenges of the teenage years hit and the kids are actively seeking social status and bonds with friends, know that they depend on you as the steady, foundational presence in their lives.

We implore you, don't let soccer performance and expectations get in the way of your relationship. Our kids don't always show it, but they need us to be Mom or Dad, not an agent.

Two Final Checklists

As we wrap up this book, we hope you've learned about the game and how to navigate the youth soccer landscape here in the USA. More importantly, we hope this book has offered tangible ways to help you along your own journey as a soccer parent.

There's certainly a lot of information to take in. We've intentionally sectioned off the book and named the chapters for ease of finding the information you want to review or reference...but we wanted to take it a step further with two checklists. The first outlines a Best Version of Self Plan for your child, which is followed up with an age specific breakdown of key developmental markers.

Next is specifically for parents, which we're calling the Practice and Game Day Routines checklist. Taking a positive approach, we wanted to share all the opportunities available to parents.

It's the quickest reference available for soccer parents. We'll leave you with these two checklists and the developmental plan instead of a chapter summary.

Best Version of Self Plan

Attribute/Years old	<6	6-10	11-14	>15
Psychological				
Joy				
Growth Mindset				
Confidence Management				
Adapability				
Technical				
Ball Handling				
First Touch				
1v1				
Ball Striking				
Tactical				
Space				
Time				
Game Models				
Superiorities				
Physical				
Agility				
Balance				
Coordination				
Speed				

The plan is a reference for parents to understand the big picture of a youth's development.

MOST IMPORTANT RULE: The kid should find joy in the game. If training is too much, then take a break. Let the child lead in the quantity of training.

For each age group, we have developed a checklist for parent and child to explore. Try these activities and see if your child enjoys and wants more. Stop doing activities that your child does not enjoy. Fostering the intrinsic desire will lead to long-term success rather than forcing soccer on children which will likely lead to failure and years of resentment.

At all ages, create an environment that is supportive both physically and mentally.

CHECKLIST

The following is a supplemental -not exhaustive- checklist to complement your player's existing soccer training. Choose those activities that make the most sense for your player given their interest and current soccer conditions.

<u>Under 6 years old</u>
At this age, it's about creating an environment of accidental play. Keep it fun...

Psychological
- Develop focus through play.
- Promote a love of learning through ball mastery.
- Bond with your child through playing soccer.

Technical
- Leave 5-6 small soccer balls around the house. Walk around the house leading a soccer ball so your child tries to walk a ball around the house.
- Create an obstacle course where they have to walk around pillows or tables.
- Have them hit the ball against a wall or sofa.
- Don't worry about ball-striking at this age.

Get a balance bike to learn how to ride a bike. The balance and strength will come in handy later. And it's fun. Tag and playground equipment offer the perfect blend of fun and athletic development as well.

<u>6-10 years old</u>
This stage is about helping your player explore the game. Engage them by playing and creating soccer spaces.

Psychological
- Introduce the Growth Mindset idea that dedication and reps lead to success while brains and talent are only a start point.
- Continue to bond with your child through play.
- Guide your child through the early stages of team play.

Technical
- Develop a space in the yard where your child can play soccer. Create goals and leave cones.
- Create a space where a wall is close by so kids can kick the ball against the wall to work on first touches.
- If your child wants, help set up soccer pick up. Parent-child pickup can be lots of fun.
- Play games where kids take on other kids or parents in 1v1.

Tactical
- Introduce the idea of moving into open space.
- Watch games in person or on TV for as long as they are interested.
- Ask questions about "individual tactics" during 1v1 and 2v2 games. "If you want to go to your right, which direction do you want to trick the defender into moving? Left, YES!"
- Introduce numeric superiority ("Which is better, the 2v1 here or the 2v3 there?") and identifying attacking spaces.

Physical
- Encourage your child to play other sports.

<u>11-14 years old</u>
Help them develop a durable mental game. Watch games with them and talk about what happened. Enable them to play pickup and other sports.

Psychological

- Check in regularly on how much your child is enjoying the game. Encourage them to take a break when needed and realistic.
- Reinforce the Growth Mindset idea that dedication and reps lead to success while brains and talent are only a start point.
- Introduce the Confidence Management concept that there will be ups and downs and the player should not let others significantly change their perceptions of themselves.
- Introduce the idea that the player must adapt to the playing conditions. Be aware enough to identify the things that work and the things that don't work.

Technical
- Ensure a time and space in the yard where your child can work on individual skills if they want.
- Enable your child to understand proper ball striking technique from their coach and the opportunity to practice next to or against a wall.
- Facilitate regular pick up or futsal if your player desires.
- Play1v1 for fun.

Tactical
- If interesting, watch games in person or on TV and talk about open space and runs for timing. Realize that most goals are scored between the 6-18 yard line.
- Continue to develop individual tactics.
- Master numerical superiorities and start to understand qualitative and socio-affective superiorities.
- Learn to generate more time on the ball by better spatial orientation, which includes manipulating the defender's positioning to "create the space you want to attack."

Physical
- Play other sports or dance.
- Buy bands to help players strengthen the ligaments/tendons in hips to prevent injuries. Do balance board work if possible.
- Girls can start speed and core work earlier if they are developing faster physiologically.

<u>15+ years old</u>
At this age, let the coaching professionals do their jobs. Be the person your child can count on for emotional support. Enable both their individualized soccer training as well as non-soccer activities.

Psychological
- Be aware of how much your player is enjoying playing and/or the challenge.
- Confidence Management is key at this stage. Do your best to keep an open dialog.
- Introduce the idea that the player should work on developing anticipation skills, most likely by watching their games on video or observing other games.

Technical
- Facilitate 1v1 attacking and defending through playing.
- Enable your player to have access to a goal and or wall for ball striking. Facilitate regular pick-up or futsal if your player desires.
- Ability to play one and two touch in a variety of scenarios.
- Add advanced striking techniques and accurate long-range distributions to the toolbox.

Tactical
- Develop a full sense of positional responsibilities.
- Understand positional rotations throughout the field, especially those pertaining to your child's own position.
- Implement all four tactical superiorities at an advanced level.
- Showcase tactical adaptability within matches, exploiting the opponent's vulnerabilities while fending off their strengths.

Physical
- Play other sports or dance if possible
- Support at home workouts by having bands, kettlebells, and dumbbells. Ensure that your child has appropriate instruction to avoid injuries and overuse.
- Help find appropriate speed work instruction.

Practice and Game Day Routines

Practices

Arrive 5 to 15 Minutes Early	
During Practice...	
-Stick around and Quietly Observe the Session	
-"Me Time", Run Errands, or Time w/ Younger Kids	
Child-Led Conversation on Ride Home	

Games

Pregame

Eat a Healthy Meal an Hour Before Activity	
Equipment Check before Leaving Home	
Arrive 5-10 Minutes before Designated Time	
Greet Other Parents and Settle; Set out Chairs	

During the Game

Cheering Good, Directing Bad	
Positive Conversations with Parents	
Let Players Play, Coaches Coach, and Refs Ref	
Plan Fun Team Bonding Activities	
Enjoy Relationships with Your Soccer Family	

Post-Game

Have a Plan for the Drive Home	
Ask if Your Child Had Fun	
Talk about the Game Only if the Child Wants to	
Sing to the Radio or Listen to a Game on the Ride	
Splurge on the Occasional Post-Game Meal or Treat	

> I do think there is the ultimate goal. This is the same thing with youth sports. We want to win the game, but if we don't know why or how, we have to now have sub-goals. It's all of these click downs that eventually get to the point where it's like, "well, we've got to be able to build out of the back, right? So in this style of play, we're going to work on building out of the back, probably going to sacrifice results, but it's not about the result right now." The end goal is something completely different. It's the same thing with the checklist, to create the habit. Maybe make the first thing you say when you arrive at a field that day something positive around the parents.
>
> -Heath Pearce

Conclusion

As with this book, your child's playing career will have a beginning, middle, and end. This book was written to provide context so you have a sense of the whole process. We encourage you to re-read this book as your player moves through the different stages as you will likely discover new applicable considerations.

The key point of the book is to let your child's intrinsic desire drive his soccer playing experience. Let them find the joy in the game. At the end of the day, the game is about kicking a ball between some sticks. Perfection is overrated as a player and parent. Getting intentional reps done - and learning from them - is the key to improvement.

On game days, give some thought to how you can be the best version of yourself and support your player. Each circumstance is unique and ranges from advice-giver to just listening and being empathetic. Do your best to not get caught up in the over-the-top emotions and antics of other parents. Celebrate what your player has done that day. Don't forget to enjoy yourself.

On the training days, enjoy getting to know other folks. It takes a village to create a great experience. Ask your player what they learned that practice.

In the big picture, soccer can teach the mindset, process, and skills needed to be successful in life. The truth is that your child will need to be 10% different in order to be successful in soccer, career, and life. It may take 10-20 years to fully understand the impact that the game can have on your children's lives.

Not every day will be a kumbaya day. There will be highs and lows. We found that creating a few good memories every week is a good way to create a pathway for your child to be the best version of themselves.

www.ingramcontent.com/pod-product-compliance
Lightning Source LLC
Chambersburg PA
CBHW051958150726
47999CB00004B/1428